Praise for **Th**

MW00577381

"*The Mind-Body Way* shares the key to cultivating a harmonious professional life, so that one's decisions, actions, and interactions confidently come from a foundation of true inner wisdom."

SHARON SALZBERG, author of
Lovingkindness and *Real Life*

"*The Mind-Body Way* is a brilliant new guide for leaders who want to discover the power of embodiment. Written by Courtney Amo, Dr. Julie Beaulac, and Casey Berglund, the book explores a new frontier in leadership: how to reduce stress, foster creativity and connection through increased body awareness. It's practical, full of good ideas, and easy to read. I recommend it for any and all leaders who want to feel increased well-being and make a bigger positive impact."

GAY HENDRICKS, PhD, author of
The Big Leap and *The Genius Zone*

"*The Mind-Body Way* is a must-read guide for anyone who wants to lead with more purpose, compassion, and resilience. This book has the power to change our individual and collective lives."

SHAUNA SHAPIRO, PhD, professor,
Santa Clara University; author of *Rewire Your Mind*
and *Good Morning, I Love You*

"We say that design thinking starts with empathy, but you have to have empathy for yourself before you can understand others. Empathy is an embodied experience, critical to living an authentic life and for being an authentic and successful leader. The authors have, for the first time, explained how the mind-body connection relates to leadership in easy-to-understand examples from life and the latest neuroscience. Read this important book—it will change the way you lead and the way you live."

"Deep kindness and wisdom pervade this book—deep enough to bring your body on board in service of your leadership, which is in service of everyone."

"Now more than ever, the world needs compassionate, aware individuals to share their gifts and step into their unique form of aligned leadership. This incredible guide holds deep wisdom and practical support to empower you to access your body's guidance and trust in the purposeful contribution the world is waiting for from you!"

"The revolutionary book *The Mind-Body Way* paves the way for a new generation of embodied leaders. Dr. Beaulac, Casey Berglund, and Courtney Amo show us that whether or not we identify as the one in charge, we can develop self-mastery through sharpening self-awareness, mindfulness, and courage. A must-have for teachers, guides, and leaders across disciplines!"

WILLA BLYTHE BAKER, author of *The Wakeful Body: Somatic Mindfulness as a Path to Freedom*

"Reading *The Mind-Body Way* reminds us that we all have an embodied wisdom. By paying attention to our bodies AND our minds, we have access to wisdom and knowing that surpasses our intellectual capacity. Full of practical applications and exercises, *The Mind-Body Way* gently guides you to explore ways of increasing your reliance on the vital mind-body connection as a path to wholeness, fulfillment, and as a vital source of information."

JOHN W. SIGMON, CEO and activist, Sigmon Leadership Solutions

"In my time documenting the wellness movement, nothing has surprised me more than the impact embodiment has on personal transformation. *The Mind-Body Way* is a powerful guide for taking our 'somatic copilots' with us into the boardroom and beyond."

CHARLIE SMITH, producer and writer of the forthcoming *Everybody Is Doing Drugs*

"*The Mind-Body Way* shows that the surest path to resilience and equanimity for any leader is through the body. Resilience and an overall sense of well-being are tragically absent for too many leaders, and Amo, Beaulac, and Berglund show us how to retrieve our bodies and, ultimately, our souls."

JERRY COLONNA, author of *Reboot: Leadership and the Art of Growing Up*

"In *The Mind-Body Way*, the authors do an amazing job bringing logic to embodiment, and embodiment to logic. The book satisfies the mind with detailed examples of how embodiment works and why it is essential. This is done in a simple way. Easy to read. Easy to understand. I'm excited to share this book with my clients. The wisdom it offers is a gift to anyone wanting to thrive in their lifetime."

CHRISSY HOLLIS, CPA, CA, entrepreneur, founder of Spirit-First Finances

"Now more than ever, we need leadership steeped in consciousness and connection to our shared humanity. *The Mind-Body Way* is the ultimate guidepost to an intentional way of conscious leadership. It teaches us that we learn collectively how to be in community with each other and connect with our bodies to define our purpose. This is an inspirational and integral piece of work."

DIANNE BONDY, international yoga and movement teacher, speaker, activist, and author of *Yoga for Everyone*

"Are you looking for an experiential resource to help intervene in the eventual manifestation of health and fitness issues in your life or work? This collaborative initiative by Amo, Beaulac, and Berglund is an excellent resource that I highly recommend. The experiential approach to address the critical topics of resilience, connection, purpose, listening to our bodies, and connecting with ourselves and others is very timely. Trust your body and what you feel; the innate wisdom will serve you well!"

DARREN DUGUAY, EFI, BSc, BEd, CD1, ND,
founder of Emotional Fitness® Academy

"We know much about the value of IQ and EQ, but there is great intelligence in the body that we are just learning to understand. The value of becoming more aware of the body and its connection to the brain is key to being the most effective creator you can be. I recommend this book for all people who want to support their self awareness, well-being, and vitality."

DIANA CHAPMAN, cofounder,
the Conscious Leadership Group

"It's difficult for leaders to get the most out of their team when they're asking too much of themselves. *The Mind-Body Way* outlines a clear and practical path toward resilience and restoration that will recenter your work and help your people reach their full potential."

DAVID BURKUS, author of *Leading from Anywhere* and the forthcoming *Best Team Ever*

"In a time when we are more disconnected and burned-out than ever, *The Mind-Body Way* offers compassionate wisdom and insight to help readers navigate the path back to embodiment so they can reconnect with their intuition and lead with intentionality. This is a book I wish had existed a decade ago when I was in chronic pain, could barely walk, and was desperately searching for a way back to myself. Amo, Beaulac, and Berglund have compiled and presented exactly the information needed by anyone who wants to learn to tap into their inner wisdom, thrive, and bring their gifts to the world."

THERESA BAILEY, national bestselling author, founder of Starfish Synergies Inc., creator of Play-Doh Power Solutions corporate training

"*The Mind-Body Way* is a compassionate deep dive into body consciousness that offers a unique perspective on the impact listening to our bodies has on becoming more balanced and effective leaders. Whether looking for better results at the workplace or wanting to create healthier relationships, this illuminating book provides solid research along with plenty of real-life examples, insightful questions, and curated exercises that infuse more awareness and intention into daily living. The reader walks away with both a broad understanding of leadership embodiment and a set of practical tools to achieve it."

RINA WELLES, lawyer and council facilitator

THE
MIND-BODY
WAY

The Embodied Leader's Path to Resilience, Connection, and Purpose

THE MIND BODY WAY

Courtney Amo · Dr. Julie Beaulac · Casey Berglund

PAGE TWO

In order to protect the privacy of individuals, composite
characters have been created to share the stories
and lived experiences of people interviewed for this book.

Cataloguing in publication information is
available from Library and Archives Canada.
ISBN 978-1-77458-360-9 (paperback)
ISBN 978-1-77458-361-6 (ebook)

Page Two
pagetwo.com

Edited by Kendra Ward
Copyedited by John Sweet
Proofread by Crissy Calhoun
Cover and interior design by Fiona Lee
Interior illustrations by Fiona Lee

mindbodywaybook.com

To you, the smart and ambitious leader
who picked up this book,

May your journey back to your body offer
you the compassion, resilience, courage, connection,
trust, and purpose of the Embodied Leader.

Now, it's your turn. We invite you to use
this space to write in your own dedication. To whom
or to what do you dedicate your journey?

_____

_____

_____

Contents

Lead from
the Inside Out

Each body comes with
a built-in, ancient knowledge
and communication system
meant to keep us safe,
healthy, and connected with
ourselves and others.

A FEW YEARS ago, Courtney was sitting on the couch in her psychologist's office, holding a weighted stuffed unicorn on her lap. Her psychologist—a warm and attentive woman with whom she'd been working for over a decade—was asking about a challenge Courtney was experiencing in her leadership role at work. "I seem to be running on empty," shared Courtney, "and I can't find my way back... you know, to how I was before."

At some point, while she was describing the situation, her psychologist stopped her and inquired, "What just happened?"

"What do you mean?" Courtney asked.

"Your body, something just happened in your body," her psychologist responded.

Courtney looked down at her torso and legs, thinking, "What is she talking about?"

Her psychologist continued, "I'm going to ask you about what is happening at work again, but this time, I don't want you to think about my question. I want you to listen to what your body is answering, and tell me about that instead."

"My stomach is knotting up," remarked Courtney, and then continued to share about a tightness and a hollowness inside. As she described these sensations, they grew stronger, louder. Then she ran out of words and started to cry.

Surprisingly, once Courtney let that happen, she felt so much relief. The tightness dissipated, and a tingling sensation moved from her stomach to her chest, throat, and shoulders. "Good work!" her psychologist said encouragingly. "Next time, we will skip all the talking and let your body speak instead."

The Mind-Body Way is about starting that kind of conversation with your own body. And if the two of you are already talking, this book will deepen the dialogue.

Why does this conversation with your body matter? Because, as a leader in today's world, you know there has to be a better way—a way to lead that is powerful, connected, and aligned with purpose; a way that nourishes you and allows you to move through massive change without burnout; that inspires and empowers others, and yourself.

When you engage in this conversation and bring your body on board, your leadership can benefit from the strength and wisdom of your whole self, including that inner guide you may have been ignoring or that you genuinely never knew you had. Say hello to your "somatic copilot," and to the experience of embodied leadership.

Leading the Mind-Body Way

As a leader, your job is to bring about results by guiding and inspiring others. As you expand in your leadership role, especially in these complex times, you may feel as though you are being stretched to do more, to be more, to consider more, and to give more. Do you ever wonder about the effectiveness of your way of leading? Are you spending your energy wisely? Or do you feel as if you are teetering on the brink of exhaustion? Reaching your full potential is difficult when you are constantly feeling overwhelmed, stressed, and possibly even sick.

So what do you do? Do you ask your body what it thinks or needs, or do you use your brain and willpower to push through, with the hope that things will get better at some point?

For many years, Julie tuned out her body's messages and pushed herself beyond healthy limits. She did this in sports, in her career, and in her relationships. In some ways, this served her well. She received scholarships and completed her doctorate in less than the average time, got into her first choice of programs for both her doctorate and her residency, did a long-distance hike despite being very ill, and cycled a challenging course for a week in Corsica, France, to the point that she lost most of the sensation in her hands. "Although I thoroughly enjoyed most of these experiences, too much of even a 'good thing' is still too much," shared Julie. Her disrespect for her body's limits, and her "push through" strategy became unworkable when she ended up in a toxic work environment. Reconnecting to her body's wisdom and bringing her body back on board allowed for a more balanced way of being. She eventually left the toxic workplace and made several other big changes in her life that altered her course forever.

Having a body is the most tangible and generalizable part of being human. We all have one. And each body comes with a built-in, ancient knowledge and communication system meant to keep us safe, healthy, and connected to ourselves and others.

Buddhist teacher and author Willa Blythe Baker reminds us that "the mind is distracted but the body is not ... the body is already mindful." Many of us have forgotten how to drop in and listen to our bodies, and no longer use this embodied wisdom to shift our mindsets and behaviors. And the consequences for our well-being, health, and effectiveness are significant.

Your ability to thrive depends in part on your capacity to tap into intuition and inner wisdom. Allowing awareness to come back into your body—or embodiment—is a way for you to reconnect and reclaim this knowledge and to break the cycle of stress and overwhelm.

Why We Need Embodied Leaders NOW

The world is facing unprecedented technological change. The years following 2020 and COVID-19 destabilized economies, institutions, and our day-to-day lives. There is significant stress about the challenges and impacts of climate change. Our minds are bombarded with information. Our nervous systems are overwhelmed and often poorly regulated. Many of us feel depleted. Our bodies are deprived of fundamental needs such as movement, connection, touch, and space to be in solitude. Many of us do not know how to calm and soothe ourselves and others. Most of us are exhausted.

How effective are we when we're drained?

Casey shares from experience that it is impossible to live harmoniously with the stresses of today's world, let alone consciously lead, without a nourished and vital body and the means to receive its brilliant wisdom. "We have to take care of our vessels and listen to what they have to say," she insists.

There is a way to cut through all this noise. There is a way to access the inner resources that can guide you through this chaotic time. You can tap into the somatic copilot that is your body. This moment, right now, presents an opportunity for a reset, and calls on you to lead yourself and others in courageous new ways.

Allowing awareness to come back into your body—or embodiment—is **a way to reconnect and to break the cycle of stress and overwhelm.**

To be clear, when we talk about leaders, we don't just mean managers, directors, or C-suite executives. Leaders are also founders, entrepreneurs, change-agents, community organizers, coaches, and parents. As a leader, you are bringing forth important outcomes for yourself, for others, and for your broader community.

More than ever, we need leaders who are authentic, aligned, and in tune with their bodies and their environments. We need leaders who connect deeply with others, are intuitive, show empathy and compassion, are inclusive, recognize the value of diversity, and can hold space in their bodies for difficult conversations. We need leaders who build and foster environments where others feel safe, secure, and able to create, innovate, and take risks.

This book is an introduction to embodiment and offers an easy-to-follow path to becoming more of an Embodied Leader. It is meant as an accessible, streamlined point of entry, and it builds on a rich knowledge tradition that we cannot fully do justice to in such a short book. As you continue to delve into embodiment, we invite you to explore the many resources that we reference.

Through current information, meaningful stories, self-reflection, and exercises that bring your body on board, this book will support you in connecting to the strength and wisdom of your whole self, so that you can do your work in the world.

Guidance for
Your Journey

Embodied leadership comes from greater embodiment, coupled with increased consciousness and intentionality in your life.

WE THREE AUTHORS are women on the Embodied Leader path ourselves. In early 2020, we came together to write this book because we believed that, individually and collectively, leadership could be done differently. We feel that more than ever now.

In the resources we engage with about leadership, the body is often left out of the equation. We observe high levels of burnout and health issues in our communities. We know leaders who do everything "right"—everything they think they "should"—but who feel drained and unfulfilled. We have been those leaders. We also know leaders who are doing things differently, and we want to learn more from them. These leaders consider the whole person when providing performance feedback; they show their emotions when discussing difficult situations; they carve out time in their busy schedules to go for a walk; they prioritize self-care— sleep, meditation, connection with their loved ones—and encourage others to do the same.

Here, we have married our understanding of embodiment practices with how leaders can become even more effective and purpose-driven in their personal lives and at work. We have had our own experiences, which we share through these pages—experiences of more traditional leadership and of the light, expansive space that is created by Embodied Leaders.

All three of us are leaders in our own personal lives and at work. We are also trained and experienced yoga instructors who have been engaged in embodiment practices for over fifty years combined. We have come to embodiment through different paths.

Julie is a registered psychologist practicing in Ottawa, Ontario. She has worked in academic and hospital settings and now has her own practice providing psychotherapy and consultation to individuals, groups, and organizations. In all areas of her work, she is passionate about optimizing well-being and leadership through embodiment.

Casey is a former registered dietitian and yoga teacher turned professional coach and embodiment guide. She is the founder of Worthy and Well, an integrative coaching and training business based in Calgary, Alberta. Through her 2019 TEDx Talk "Let Your Body Lead," and the private and group coaching programs she has created and facilitated online, Casey has helped thousands of people work with the wisdom of their bodies to create powerful, purpose-driven lives and businesses.

Courtney is a public sector leader and founder of Mahaa, an independent yoga, wellness retreat, lifestyle coaching, and consulting practice based in Moncton, New Brunswick. She has a background in psychology, program evaluation, and facilitation, and over twenty years of yoga teaching and public sector leadership experience. Across her many roles, Courtney helps people approach work, life, and well-being from an embodied perspective.

While we have each experienced instances of privilege, trauma, empowerment, and disempowerment, as able-bodied white women, it is impossible for us to speak from the lived experiences of all, particularly those who deal with systemic oppression on a daily basis. We have done our best to bring those perspectives to this book by interviewing a diverse range of incredible leaders who have lived different experiences in their bodies, and who were willing to share their insights with us.

To respect the privacy of these individuals, we have created composite "characters" as vehicles to share their stories. You will be introduced to Carrie, Andrew, Melissa, Jesse, Dalila, and Darshan, who vary in their professional backgrounds. A few are entrepreneurs, two are executives, one is a community organizer, and one is a performer. While their contexts may be different, they are all leaders in their own right. We hope that their stories will resonate with you and your own unique lived experience.

Your Embodied Leader Journey

No matter your role, embodiment can help you leverage discomfort, optimize stamina, and find meaningful success in life and leadership.

Leadership is not about one way of being—it is a journey that evolves as you go and grow.

To support your journey, we have organized this book around six broad pillars:

Pillar 1: Building Body Awareness and Compassion

Pillar 2: Working with Your Mind-Body and Nervous System

Pillar 3: Taking Risks and Practicing Courage

Pillar 4: Consciously Connecting with Yourself and Others

Pillar 5: Trusting and Integrating Body Wisdom

Pillar 6: Finding Purpose and Contribution

Together, these pillars foster a more embodied approach to leadership. Rather than think of them as a linear path, it can be helpful to visualize them as an interconnected whole, as in the diagram opposite. The first two pillars are at the center of the diagram to emphasize their importance as the starting point and core of the journey. The remaining pillars surround the core and extend out, to show how growth within each of these pillars contributes to growth across all of them, and leads to greater levels of embodiment. Embodied leadership comes from greater embodiment, coupled with increased consciousness and intentionality in your life.

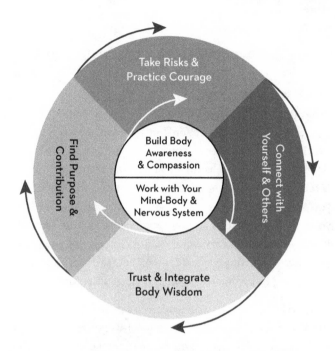

We have also identified three Embodied Leader styles—Explorer, Connector, and Integrator—to help you characterize your current state of embodiment. These styles are not experienced in a linear progression. You may identify with different styles in different contexts, or you may identify with more than one style at a time.

The three Embodied Leader styles are described on the following pages. We give you leadership examples to make each style more concrete. The stories we share in each pillar will provide further examples, and help you imagine living and leading with greater embodiment. You will learn how each of the characters presented in each pillar has experienced these styles, and what they have learned along the way.

Embodied Leader Styles

Explorer

What it might feel like. You know the importance of self-awareness and self-reflection, but you may not always practice them. You can sense signals from your body, but you don't always stop to listen, or understand what your body is telling you. You have a sense of what body wisdom is, but you sometimes ignore your instincts. You can be hard on yourself, especially when you make mistakes. You may find it difficult to set and hold boundaries. Sometimes your emotions get ahead of you. You can feel yourself disconnecting or wanting to protect yourself in difficult situations.

Leadership example. You are an executive presenting to the board of directors. As you get to your recommendations, you feel that the energy in the room has changed. You notice anxiety rising in your body, but you push through and ignore what is happening in the room. When board members start to speak, you are surprised by their reactions to your recommendations. You are left feeling as if you missed something important, but you are not sure what. You leave the office without talking to anyone. That night, you have trouble sleeping, and you struggle with fatigue and pain in your body the next day.

Connector

What it might feel like. You practice self-reflection. You are aware of physical sensations in your body and what they might mean. You listen and work to meet your body's needs. You generally trust your body's wisdom, and take actions based on what your body is signaling. You have a calming presence, and people feel safe around you. You have a healthy sense of boundaries. You can feel emotions rise in you and allow them to pass. You work to stay present in your body when faced with difficult situations.

Leadership example. You are an entrepreneur negotiating an important contract with a service provider. Something about how they are responding to your questions is triggering a reaction in you. You can feel your heart beating a bit faster. You sense that adrenaline is making you more alert and energized. You notice this, and start breathing more consciously. You wait until the reaction stabilizes, and you tell the service provider that you will require more information from them on this issue before you can continue the conversation. When you follow up with your business partner, they remind you of past issues with the service provider's performance. You feel embarrassed for forgetting, but quickly rebound into gratitude because your partner has your back. You can now go back to the negotiation with more specific questions to mitigate any future risks to your business.

Integrator
What it might feel like. You have daily practices that allow you to connect to your body, yourself, and others. You are in tune with your body, and act on its signals. You use your body's wisdom to support you in your decisions. You model openness, trust, and vulnerability, and you embody your

values. You have strong but flexible boundaries. You can regulate your emotions, and stay present in your body when faced with difficult situations.

Leadership example. You are the head of a nonprofit organization and are faced with the need to cut back on services. To make the best possible decision, you engage with your team members to get their advice, while being forthright about the implications. You share about the difficulty of these decisions, and show that you can feel strong emotions without them overwhelming you. Some of your team members approach you with fear about what this will mean for them, and you hold space for those conversations with empathy, clarity, and transparency. For some team members, the uncertainty is too much and they choose to look for other work. For others, your trust in their advice makes them more engaged; they want to find solutions with you. Through this stressful time, you maintain your daily practices, communicate, stay connected to your team, and pay attention to your body's signals.

What about You?

Now, what about you? To what extent do you identify with one or more of these styles? When have you felt this way in your body? Try not to overthink your answers—the first response that comes up is often the right one for right now.

Whatever style you tend to show up as, there is no need to worry or judge yourself. Most of us are operating from the Explorer style, at least some of the time, and there are benefits to this style that we will explore later. You will learn to build from Explorer and start to experience and integrate the characteristics of the other Embodied Leader styles.

Even Integrators need to do this work—sometimes just to get out of their comfort zones! Each style has room to explore and grow. By learning about all the styles, you may find that you are better able to maintain or come back to embodiment when you are faced with different contexts and challenges. You will also likely find that you are better able to support those around you in becoming more embodied themselves.

Where This Journey Might Take You

Where you begin and end on this journey is up to you and the circumstances of your life. You can expect to experience a wide range of benefits. You will:

- Be less of a jerk to yourself when life and leadership get difficult. You'll treat yourself with more kindness and respect through becoming aware of your body and learning how to meet uncomfortable sensations with compassion, even when you're tempted to judge.

- Receive constructive feedback from your team in an important meeting and respond with more grace, rather than becoming defensive and reactive, even though you feel your heart rate increase and your armpits sweat.

- Share new ideas that will help you grow and innovate, rather than playing it safe, even when fear wants to keep you in your comfort zone.

- Let down your guard and lead with a level of authenticity that inspires others to share when they are going through a hard time, or celebrate a big win in their personal lives. That level of connection will enhance the way you collaborate at work. You'll help others feel more allowed, alive, and whole through your presence and the energy you embody.

- Deeply trust yourself to make important life and leadership decisions, without second-guessing, even when those decisions hold a lot of weight or go against the grain. You'll trust others, too, and integrate their wisdom in your process.

- Get out of bed each morning with energy and excitement to go to work, rather than feeling exhausted, because you know you're living in alignment with a sense of purpose and serving others in a meaningful way.

No matter where you start, you can grow and find purpose in life and leadership. You can create a life full of meaning and satisfaction, where you harness and apply your gifts. You can act in alignment with what serves you and, ultimately, your own little corner of the world. You can be the Embodied Leader that is needed for our times *and* live a truly meaningful, purpose-driven life.

The Path of Least (or Most) Resistance

On this journey, you will have moments of resistance. You will try to grasp for control and safety. At times, doing what your body is asking you to do will be totally disruptive to your life. It will take time to learn the language of feeling and sensation, to hear the voice of intuition and inner knowing, and to trust your own body's wisdom. There will be moments that feel unusual and uncomfortable. Growth creates some discomfort.

————————

Discomfort often provides the greatest opportunity
for remembering, and for waking up to what is.

————————

Discomfort often provides the greatest opportunity for remembering, and for waking up to what is. If you want to really show up and be present, you need to be willing to get out of your comfort zone. To hold space for happiness, joy, and expansion. To stay connected through sadness, anger, and contraction. Staying with and creating opportunities for discomfort leads to personal growth and transformation.

Embodiment is staying in your body even when you want to hop out.

In hot yoga, they tell us to stay in the room, even when it gets "hot." We are certain you have your own examples of when things get "hot": when a conversation gets particularly difficult and you or the other person tries to break off and leave the room; when your body is flooded with emotions and you feel a strong urge to distract or numb yourself, by scrolling on your device, reaching for a snack when you're not hungry, or watching something mindless; when you are called out in a meeting and wish your body would turn invisible.

Staying in your body can be hard. It is okay, and even helpful, to come into and out of embodiment. We will say more about this later. The key is to do so with greater degrees of awareness and intention.

Starting Your Journey

We encourage you to take your time with this book. In the words of Sharon Salzberg, "It's not a race, you know." We see this journey as containing three main components: awareness, self-reflection, and experimentation. Each pillar is designed around these components, and can be read in approximately fifteen to twenty minutes, with exercises taking another ten minutes or so. If you wanted to, you could read the whole book over the course of a week. Or you could invest thirty minutes and work through one pillar per week. It's up to you.

Self-reflection and experimentation through deliberate practice are what make leadership training work. We suggest that you keep a journal as you work through the book to capture insights, questions, and observations. Try the exercises, and adapt them to make them your own. Bringing your body on board will lead to changes in your life, and you get to choose how much change and when.

As you engage fully with the material here, you will notice shifts in how you view your body, yourself, and your leadership role. You will begin to lead more from the inside out. Although you control the pace of change, a fair warning: once you become more embodied, there is no turning back. However, as one leader we worked with put it, "I haven't ever heard anyone regret going down the path of becoming more embodied, ever."

Exercises to Bring Your Body on Board

Each pillar of the book contains a set of concrete exercises that will support you in integrating your learning and expanding your connection to yourself and others. A first set of exercises is included below to launch you on your journey.

Sensing your body
Come into a comfortable standing, sitting, or lying-down position.

Choose one place in your body that you can safely and comfortably bring your attention to. For instance, you may bring your attention to your right knee, as though you were observing every detail of it from the inside.

Get curious about this place in your body and notice the subtle and maybe not so subtle sensations that reside there.

Maybe you sense some pain in your right knee, and when you feel more closely into it, the pain feels dull, and there is a heaviness there.

Spend some time exploring and describing what you are noticing, feeling, sensing.

Sensing your intention

For this exercise, we suggest recording your answers with a pen and paper, but you may prefer to use an electronic device.

Choose a position that calls to you; it may be sitting, squatting, or standing.

Ask yourself, "What do I hope to take away from this journey?" Write down the first response that comes to mind. Resist the urge to overthink it.

Pause, breathe, read your answer out loud, and notice what sensations come up in your body. Note those sensations next to your answer—for example, "tightness in my throat," "expansiveness in my chest." If you do not notice any sensations, that is okay. You can note that too.

Now ask yourself, "What is important to me about this journey?" Again, write down your answer, read it out loud, and notice whatever sensations arise in your body.

Ask yourself, "Why is that important?" Reflect, write, sense, capture... and ask yourself this question a few more times until your body tells you that you are done.

We suggest that you write your most fundamental "why" on the first page of the book, as a reminder.

Sharing your intention

Choose a trusted person to share with. Verbalize to this person what sensations came up in your body during the exercise above and as you worked on your intention and your more fundamental "why." Describe these sensations in as much detail as possible. If you did not notice sensations, you can share this too.

Encourage your friend or partner to ask clarifying questions, to help you dig deeper into your own understanding.

Pay particular attention to what sensations come up in your body as you share your story.

Close the session with a thank-you and a hug or other form of touch or connection, as feels appropriate.

PILLAR 1

Building Body Awareness and Compassion

Embodiment is the ability to feel your feelings and draw from them the data your body is sending. **It is about sensing, not thinking.**

CARRIE USES HER body for a living. Her leadership spans interesting domains. She is a tech entrepreneur turned professional circus performer who—in the first five minutes of being interviewed for this book—apologized for her fuzzy thoughts. They were the result of post-concussion symptoms. She had a bad fall in rehearsal. "I knew I shouldn't have been up there that day," she said. "I felt off, but I pushed through. I did a trick at the front of a swing, and when I should have caught my legs, I missed, and landed hard. The physio told me I definitely had a concussion. I told her I was fine, and then went to a dance class afterward. The next day, I felt awful. And here we are."

Carrie embodies the Explorer style in this example. She knows the importance of self-awareness and self-reflection, especially given the risks she takes in her work, but she lets her self-reflective practices slide when she's busy. Maybe you can relate? The day she fell, she sensed a signal from her body, but she didn't pause and truly pay attention. She ignored her instinct, and it cost her.

Just like Carrie, you use your body for a living. Although you may not be a circus performer, a dancer, or an Olympian, your body is the means through which you experience the world. As a leader, you cannot be effective in the roles you play when you lack awareness of how your body is trying to communicate with you, or when you ignore or misjudge the messages you receive after finally tuning in.

You cannot be an effective leader when you lack awareness of how your body communicates with you, or when you ignore or misjudge its messages.

Carrie's concussion reminded her of the importance of caring for her body and listening to its wisdom. In addition, she felt that she was being forced to learn how to have compassion for herself. In many ways, her accident propelled her into the Connector style and will help her journey to the Integrator. As with many smart, ambitious, and high-achieving leaders, Carrie's default reaction to her accident was to beat herself up for making such a big mistake and paying for it. Building a practice of self-compassion— choosing to be kind to herself, despite the mistake—has been an important part of her Embodied Leader path.

We invite you to reconnect with your body in a kind and compassionate way. We encourage you to get to know yourself more deeply so that trust can be rebuilt, and the lines of communication between your mind and your body can be unhindered. Increased body awareness will not only help you meet your body's needs and support your well-being, it will also help you engage in conversation with your body as you would with a close friend or ally. When you think of your body as your somatic copilot—the internal guide you have either been ignoring or that you genuinely never knew you had—you can achieve your goals in life and leadership in a more effective, integrated, and sustainable way.

This pillar is about building awareness of your body, which is a prerequisite for the deeper embodiment work you will undertake on this journey. We explore embodiment and disembodiment, as well as help you get a feel for these different states. We also discuss mindfulness, emotional competence, and compassion. We then tie these concepts back to being in your body, and what that might mean in life and in leadership.

So What Is Embodiment?

To best explain embodiment, let's start with mindfulness.

You have likely heard of the benefits of mindfulness—of focusing your attention on the present moment, of acknowledging and accepting that moment, without judgment. The Pali word for mindfulness is *sati*, and it means "remembering." When you are mindful, you are better aware of what is driving you, what is happening within and around you, and what is important. Mindfulness builds an inner sense of knowing and allows you to tap into your insights and inner wisdom.

Julie learned about mindfulness through yoga. Courtney introduced her to yoga in 2002, and at first the final resting pose was the most challenging for her. "Just lie there? Do *nothing*?" she thought. "My mind reviewed my to-do lists, and I felt uncomfortable and agitated. In the beginning, I didn't fully get the point, but I stayed committed." By 2017, Julie took part in her first eleven-day silent vipassana meditation retreat. There were many moments of discomfort during those long days of sitting in silence. But she grew to accept the discomfort, and through practicing mindfulness she even experienced moments of bliss and great insight.

Over the past few years, scientific and cultural interest in mindfulness has exploded. Mindfulness teaching and practice are showing up in our workplaces, schools, health centers, and communities. Programs have been developed to help people incorporate mindfulness into their daily lives, promoting benefits such as reduced emotional reactivity and burnout, decreased stress and anxiety, improved relationships and compassion, as well as enhanced overall well-being.

This expanded interest has occurred for good reason: being present matters. But what if mindfulness is not enough?

If mindfulness is being fully aware of the present moment, of our thoughts, feelings, and bodily sensations, we like to think of embodiment as *mindfulness turned onto itself*. Embodiment is not a cognitive process. It is the integrated mind-body being more aware of itself, and ultimately using this awareness to its own benefit.

Embodiment invites a deep attunement to the "awareness of our direct sensory, mental, and emotional experience."

Richard Strozzi-Heckler, founder of the Strozzi Institute and originator of embodied leadership and somatic coaching, calls the body "the shape of our experience" and reminds us that "this shape affects the world and the world affects our shape" and that "your entire intelligence is experienced as a coherent unity attuned to the world."

Julie has developed a practice of tuning into her "felt sense"—or internal bodily awareness—and paying less attention to cognitive "noise." We say more about felt sense in Pillar 2. We can all develop this greater awareness of felt sense. "As I listened more to my felt sense," shared Julie, "I stopped ignoring or silencing my body's screams for movement." She began to sit near the back of meeting rooms so that she could do a mix of standing, squatting, and sitting on the floor. Her behavior certainly received attention, as anything different does, but the most common comment was one reflecting curiosity or generosity: "Would you like a chair?" Sometimes, she even had company.

Embodiment is a type of visceral intelligence—an intelligence felt deeply in the body that can enhance our understanding of how the body and brain are integrated and interdependent. Carrie—the tech entrepreneur and circus performer we introduced you to earlier in this chapter—experienced that visceral intelligence. She knew that something "felt off," she just didn't fully listen. Embodiment goes beyond thoughts. In fact, it is not really about thoughts. Embodiment is the ability to not only feel what you are feeling but draw from those feelings the data that your body is sending to you. It is about sensing rather than thinking.

Embodiment is accurately experiencing the inside and outside worlds at a somatic level. Connecting with an experience at a purely cognitive level is not sufficient. Bessel van der Kolk, traumatic stress clinician, researcher, and author of *The Body Keeps the Score*, describes our core experiences of ourselves as "somatic," meaning that we experience ourselves through the body, through our physicality. Embodiment is not an on-off switch, but rather a state that falls along a spectrum, from disembodiment to embodiment.

A concept related to embodiment is interoception, or interoceptive awareness, which is the body's capacity to feel itself from the inside out. For example, when you feel that your heart rate is increasing, or you feel that you need to take a deep breath, that is interoceptive awareness. Psychiatrist, neuroscientist, and originator of polyvagal theory Stephen Porges refers to interoception as the "infant's sixth sense." You will learn more about polyvagal theory in Pillar 2. Being able to sense your body is crucial to responding effectively across situations, and is linked to reduced risk for various health conditions, including depression, anxiety, and addiction. In Carrie's case, greater interoceptive awareness could have also saved her from a concussion.

Embodiment is not about working really hard to change your body. It is not about wishing your body were different—such habits tend to lead to more disembodied states of being. Rather, embodiment requires us to acknowledge and confront challenges, particularly related to our internal experiences. Doing so is not easy, and for this reason, resisting embodiment is very common and at times very necessary. We all resist it. We will say more about this a bit later.

Experiences of Embodiment

What does embodiment look and feel like for you?

For Courtney, embodiment looks like being highly attuned to the cues associated with increased anxiety, and being able to take actions that will make her nervous system feel safe again so that she can deliver that presentation or have that difficult conversation.

Embodiment for Julie looks like noticing her current state and asking, "Am I feeling rested and energized? Frantic and time pressured? Completely overwhelmed?" It then means choosing what she needs to do to get back to a more optimal state. It involves saying no, even when she feels bad about it because she may be letting someone down. It involves a shift in focus from surviving to thriving. Instead of asking herself, "How can I make this work?" she asks, "How am I nourishing myself?"

Embodiment for Casey means paying attention to her breath, observing the sensations she feels in her physical self, and then engaging in a process of gentle inquiry to illuminate what wisdom those sensations hold about what she needs. She often feels stress in her back, neck, and shoulders, and when she notices it, pays attention, and asks what that tension needs so that it can be released, she can support herself through taking a break, moving a little, or engaging in an intentional activity, such as breathwork or a bike ride.

For many, meditation, movement, and nature are direct gateways to embodiment, in addition to activities that bring them joy. Carrie shared with us, "I probably feel the most embodied when I'm in nature, either on a canoe trip or hiking. That's when I feel at my very, very best."

Embodiment can be felt in others—we can tell when others are emotionally present and aware of their bodies. It is easy to be around people who are embodied. You may recall being around someone and thinking, "Wow, that person is really comfortable in their own skin." What you may not have thought about is the extent to which that comfort and ease may have been earned through committed practice—the result of a long journey of mindfulness, embodiment work, self-awareness, and self-compassion, a journey that never really ends.

Embodiment maximizes focus and enjoyment, whether the activity is taking time in nature or collaborating on a project. For this reason, embodiment has been linked to "flow states" or being in "the zone." When we have clear goals, are pursuing an adequate level of challenge, are receiving immediate feedback, and are fully aware, safe, and secure in our bodies, we can more easily enter and stay in a flow state, either by ourselves or with others. We will say more about the link between embodiment and flow states in Pillars 4 and 6.

How many of your waking hours do you spend in embodied states compared with more disembodied states? What are the conditions or practices that help you get in "the zone" or in "flow"?

Almost all the leaders we interviewed reported the importance of some sort of mindfulness practice to help them return to, and then stay connected to, their bodies. They also spoke of embodiment as a "process" or as something that you have to train for. For instance, you might recognize that a certain type of music brings you into your body, and into a state of mind where you feel in sync and ready to work. Then you might repeat that practice, playing that music, every time you need to achieve that state.

How Disembodiment Serves (and Doesn't Serve)

Embodiment is a gradual process of coming back into the body, with safety. This book explores the impact of disembodiment, and provides you with exercises that will support a more embodied way of living and leading.

But we all resist embodiment to some extent, partly because disembodiment serves its purposes too.

Being in a disembodied state may prevent us from recognizing stress, and from actively processing and releasing that stress before it can cause harm.

As humans, we enter the world embodied. Most of the people we spoke with for this book, including Carrie, shared that they felt most connected to their bodies as children. During this time in our development, we have a clearer sense of what our needs are, a less filtered ability to express those needs, and an innate capacity to be authentic. Babies, for example, cry for milk when they are hungry and stop feeding when they are full. A toddler verbally expresses what their body needs to their caregivers, and develops a felt sense of safety and security from having those needs acknowledged and met.

For many of us, however, the journey to adulthood gradually moves us from body to head. Our culture teaches us that certain ways of knowing are better than others—such as using our brain instead of our body to interpret the world. At certain points in our lives, experience teaches us that our body is not safe, good, or valuable. We learn that our body is a liability. In trying to "fit in" with our family, community, or peer group, we may take on the thoughts and behaviors of the group rather than tapping into our own body's data. Over time, disembodiment becomes the default state of being, and the body goes into autopilot—it reacts automatically. Trauma accelerates this process of disembodiment.

Our bodies do this for a reason. Disembodiment is an adaptive outcome, the natural response of accommodating certain circumstances, especially threatening ones.

According to Stephen Porges, when faced with real or perceived threats in your environment, your nervous system may begin to associate those threats with extreme danger, even when the threats are not an actual risk. For instance, although disagreeing with your boss may be a normal part of your job, your body may perceive that disagreement as a real danger, and trigger a stress response that is designed to survive a threat. Over time, if, like an alarm system, the stress response keeps going off, you may dissociate or detach from your body as a protective mechanism.

Disembodiment may also serve you when you are trying to conserve energy and attention, allowing your autopilot response to kick in to get things done without you having to pay much attention. Well-established habits allow for the conservation of energy. The nervous system may also choose disembodiment when you are dealing with intense or chronic physical pain, or when emotional or psychological distress goes beyond what the body feels it can process.

It is neither possible nor ideal to maintain an embodied state at all times. The key is to be able to consciously choose, to discern what state will serve you best in a given situation. And to respect the need at times to not be in your body. When you can move between states with awareness and intention, you can harness the benefits of each state while mitigating the negative effects of disembodiment, such as feeling disconnected from yourself and others.

Many of the leaders we spoke with shared about how they came to realize the need for embodiment, or about accidentally arriving at embodiment. Often an injury or a health issue will sound the alarm. Carrie's concussion reminded her to listen to the cues of her body. For some, the body's alarm in advance of calamity is hard to hear, and so it is difficult to notice it and act accordingly. For others, the alarm is crystal clear, and there is an immediate shift in focus to what really matters. To connect more deeply with their body's needs, these leaders spoke about exploring different modalities such as breathwork, yoga, movement practices, body work, and reflective practices, which could include coaching, psychotherapy, and journaling. Many of the people we spoke with expressed that these modalities were transformative, beyond just healing the body.

The modalities supported people in witnessing their internal experiences and in unifying their body and mind, leading to a more embodied, integrated whole.

Emotional Competence and Embodiment

Imagine you feel the pressure of heavy workload and never-ending deadlines. There is a part of you that is aware that you cannot sustain the long work hours, skipping lunch and breaks, and the constant pressure you feel without a significant cost to you and to those around you. And yet you keep pushing through. To pause would be to admit "defeat," to face those feelings of not being good enough, of not being able to do it all, of being an impostor. Most of us experience this fear at some point, and when it comes up, it's common to run from it.

Avoiding our internal experiences—or *experiential avoidance*—is a common pitfall at the core of many health challenges. Experiential avoidance has contributed to the skyrocketing of anxiety, depression, and other health issues in higher-income countries. It is a detriment not only to our individual well-being but also to our relationships. We cannot show up or be present with others if we are not able to show up for ourselves.

There are many reasons why some of us don't have full access to our internal experiences. Our lives may involve experiences that have made it unsafe to feel or express emotions. And as we discussed earlier, we are designed to choose behaviors that will keep us safe in any given moment.

Casey has been on a lifelong journey of embracing her sensitivity, her emotions, and her empathic nature. She divulged: "I was one of those kids you couldn't lie to, because I felt and sensed what was true. When emotions in my family weren't expressed, I'd absorb them anyways. I could feel them and would internalize them. And then in moments when I needed to let it all out and I expressed my own emotions, I was often hushed." So, early on, she felt that her feelings were "too much" and therefore needed to be repressed. But in repressing them, she inhibited her own well-being and cut off the part of her that could use her empathic nature for good by deeply understanding others and leading with care.

Maybe you can relate?

Stress is an internal experience that many leaders are quite familiar with. Stress is a natural part of being human, and certainly an expected part of being a leader. In his book *When the Body Says No*, addiction, trauma, and stress expert Gabor Maté highlights that many of us have become so accustomed to stress that its absence creates unease. We are, however, learning more and more about the negative physical and psychological impacts of retaining stress in the body. Being in a disembodied state may prevent us from recognizing that we are experiencing stress, and from actively processing and releasing that stress before it can cause harm.

In leadership and management circles, you may hear a lot about emotional intelligence—your understanding of inter- and intrapersonal relations that can help you successfully adapt to your environment. Gabor Maté explores the related concept of emotional competence, or the capacity to feel, label, express, and process your emotions. Emotional competence plays a critical role in releasing stress from the body and in reducing its significant risk to your health.

Although emotional intelligence is important, without emotional competence you risk suppressing emotions, or not letting the body complete its cycle of emotional processing. It is like knowledge without practice. Blocking the processing cycle creates stress in the body, disrupts your homeostasis or equilibrium, and can lead to problems down the road.

One way to help your body complete its cycle of emotional processing is to take the time to name or label your emotions. This helps you see a thought as a thought and see that you are not your thoughts. The same is true for feelings or other internal experiences. When you put words to your feelings, activity in your brain shifts from the amygdala, which is responsible for our fear response and protecting us from danger, to the prefrontal cortex, which is responsible for inhibiting behaviors and processing emotions. When you say how you feel, you allow the rational brain to kick in and start the process of understanding—combining thinking and feeling—so that you can defuse the stress in your body. Naming or labeling also helps to build awareness of your own emotions and the emotions of others.

Compassion and Embodiment

As you become more embodied, you will grow more aware of and in tune with your body. This process is likely to bring up feelings, emotions, stories, beliefs, defense mechanisms, and more. These won't always be easy to tackle. For instance, Courtney expressed: "When I am faced with a very difficult decision, my go-to mechanism for ending the discomfort is food. At the office, people used to joke that they could tell how rough my day had been by how many little dark-chocolate wrappers were in my wastebasket." But embodiment has taught her that when she numbs her discomfort, she shuts down her emotional response and is no longer leading with her whole self. Courtney added: "When I use food to soothe my discomfort, I am ignoring important information from my body that could support me in my decision. On top of that, if I shame myself for my behavior, I create further dissonance within myself, which limits my effectiveness and my well-being."

A key practice to shift unhelpful behaviors and to hold space for what is going on in your body is compassion. By practicing compassion toward yourself, you become your own ally, providing yourself with support to keep going.

Self-compassion pioneers Kristin Neff and Christopher Germer identify three elements to self-compassion in their Mindful Self-Compassion approach:

- self-kindness (being caring, supportive, and encouraging toward yourself; offering unconditional acceptance);

- common humanity (a sense of interconnectedness, a recognition that we are all works in progress); and

- mindfulness (being aware of moment-to-moment experience, open to the present moment without resistance or avoidance).

In his compassion-focused therapy approach, psychologist Paul Gilbert, founder and president of the Compassionate Mind Foundation, distinguishes between compassion directed inward and compassion directed outward. When compassion is directed inward, that might look like deciding to go to bed on time even if you haven't finished all the tasks you wanted to accomplish that evening. When compassion is directed outward, that might look like reaching out to a colleague after a particularly difficult meeting to give them space to debrief and reflect.

Common among the different compassion approaches is the science-backed belief that kindness, both for yourself and for others, is a skill that you can grow. Carrie's compassion practice supported her in healing from her concussion and set her up to take a gentler approach the next time she makes a mistake.

Unfortunately, self-compassion is not directly valued in many cultures and is fraught with negative associations, such as selfishness, self-pity, and weakness. These unhelpful and incorrect perceptions block us from the well-being benefits of self-compassion and from a more fulsome connection to ourselves. Practicing compassion toward yourself rewires your brain to make you a better leader. It grows emotional intelligence, conscientiousness, and resilience, and it fosters a growth mindset. As well, it creates greater compassion, psychological safety—defined by psychologist Amy Edmondson as an absence of interpersonal fear—and trust within teams.

Embodiment takes compassion, and compassion takes courage. In the words of renowned meditation teacher and psychologist Jack Kornfield, "healing starts by simply becoming mindful of the body as it is." Embodiment is about having the courage to get into your body in a way that works for you, and coming back to your body time and time again so that you can build trust and grow awareness of comfort and discomfort. Embodiment is also about approaching what you discover with grace and compassion, and getting curious about how your body communicates with you about what it needs. Embodiment requires that you acknowledge and allow your felt experience with compassionate curiosity.

Showing up with awareness and compassion in your life is an ongoing process. The time and place to begin is exactly where you are right now. It will help to remember that the goal is not perfection. The goal is being whole, and living in that integrity.

Exercises to Bring Your Body on Board

Building body awareness

Sit or lie down comfortably. Place your index and middle finger at your wrist or at your neck to feel your pulse.

Bring your awareness to your beating heart, picturing it in your chest, and visualizing the blood flowing through your veins.

Notice your breathing. Count the number of seconds it takes for you to inhale, and the number of seconds it takes for you to exhale. No matter the number, see if you can gently extend your exhale to twice the length of your inhale. For example, you could inhale for two seconds and exhale for four seconds. Take your time.

Notice any changes to how you feel in your body as a result of this breathing pattern.

After a few moments, bring your awareness back to your surroundings, and stretch out your body in whatever way feels nourishing to you.

Building kindness toward yourself

Bring to mind a memory in which you experienced difficult feelings, such as fear, shame, sadness, or anger.

Allow yourself to imagine the scenario and to feel the emotions and sensations as they show up in your body.

Stay with the sensations as you are able, while speaking to yourself with kindness. You may consider also offering yourself a caring gesture, like placing your hand over your heart. Remind yourself that all sensations are welcome and that you are not your emotions.

Check in with yourself and ask your body what it needs right now.

Respond as you are able and notice any shift in how you feel.

Committing to self-care practices

Building on what you are learning about yourself through self-reflection, choose self-care practices that best meet your needs in any given moment. For instance, if you are feeling wired from a stressful day at work, you might ask a friend to take a walk with you after supper.

Self-care practices can include movement, such as walking or yoga; self-reflection, through meditation or journaling; enjoying art, music, or a good book; eating nourishing food; spending time in good company; taking care of your body, by having a bath, treating yourself to a massage, or taking a nap; and more.

Commit to noticing when more self-care would be helpful, and start by implementing at least one more self-care practice per week, with the idea of working up to at least one practice per day.

Working with Your Mind-Body and Nervous System

Resilience is a virtuous cycle. The more resilient you and others around you are, the more resilience will grow.

YEARS AGO, CASEY began guiding Andrew—a type A executive in a corporate finance role—through private yoga classes, because he'd heard the practice could help his work-related insomnia and anxiety, and promote his sharpness of mind. As someone who constantly strives to maximize his potential, he was curious about how yoga could help him become a less stressed and more powerful version of himself, in addition to relieving some of his aches and pains. Andrew began his journey as the Explorer. Even though he thought that he was connected with his body because he worked out, he hadn't tapped into his body's potential to support him in practical ways in his leadership role. He was reactive in meetings, uncertain how to release stress after a long day at work, and, of course, was having trouble sleeping. Over time, Andrew realized the additional benefits of being in his body, and continued on his path, embodying the Connector and then eventually the Integrator.

For example, instead of always being in a rush, he started to take time to get to know the people he worked with in a more personal way, which added context to the patterns he was noticing in their work. He became more authentic, never losing his strong personality, but leaning into sharing more of himself with others, even in an environment not conducive to vulnerability. He also started to ask deep questions about who he was, and where he could have the most impact with the resources he had access to.

When Casey interviewed him for this book, she could tell he had been in a reflective mood. He positioned his Zoom camera so she could see the collection of leadership books behind him. "I've read them all, Casey," he told her, "and there's nothing in those books about how to tap into the deeper wisdom of your body to tackle the bigger stresses of leading a team in a high-pressure environment. Where's the information in those books about how to lead when you're having a hard enough time falling asleep at night because your mind is spinning with thoughts about the important meeting you have the next day? Where's the wisdom about not flying off the handle when you're triggered by your team? Or not avoiding a conversation with your spouse when they're annoyed by how much you work?" He paused and added, "Remember when I struggled with all that? I mean, I'm not perfect—I still lose it sometimes—but a lot has changed. I'm way more Zen than I used to be."

This pillar is about deepening your understanding of the integrated mind-body organism that is YOU, so that you, like Andrew, can embrace a more "Zen-like" way of leading, instead of feeling plagued by stress.

In support of this, we give you a high-level primer on the nervous system. We also introduce you to polyvagal theory, to offer insights into how your nervous system and the nervous systems of those around you influence your experiences and your engagement with the world.

Building on this knowledge, and what you learned in Pillar 1, we also encourage you to reflect on your current level of mind-body self-mastery. You will begin to work with your nervous system to elevate your capacity to experience more, with greater resilience, in your life and leadership. By creating a sense of safety in your nervous system, you will grow your ability to handle the stressors of life, safeguard yourself against burnout and unhealthy relationships, and optimize satisfaction across the different domains of your life.

With this deeper, experiential understanding, you will better connect to, and become more in sync with, your mind-body, and be better able to respond to its needs.

In psychology, the term "attunement" describes a state of being connected to and in sync with someone else's feelings, in which you can recognize and respond appropriately to those feelings. When you are in sync with your own mind-body, you experience *attunement with yourself.* Through this "self-attunement," you will be more present to your needs, more authentic in your leadership, and better able to support your well-being and that of those around you.

A Case of False Dichotomies

When you think about your own body, do you think of it as a whole, complex, integrated organism, or as a bunch of parts working together? Do you see your body as an extension of your mind, or as separate from it? To what extent do you perceive your thoughts as affecting the activities of your cells?

Thinking around the mind-body has evolved quite a bit in recent years. There is now greater recognition that the mind-body operates as one, and not as separate entities, and we are moving away from false dichotomies that no longer serve our current need for greater understanding of our overall mind-body organism.

Research also suggests that brain function does not go downhill from the age of thirty, as used to be commonly believed, but that neuroplasticity is still present in the aging brain and that aging doesn't automatically lead to downward functioning. Julie likes to remind her father, who frequently uses his age as an excuse not to do things, "Dad, you get good at what you practice." Practice supports neuroplasticity, which allows you to grow into who you want to be and how you want to live and lead.

The usual understanding of leadership is also filled with false dichotomies. When we make decisions with our heads and ignore our hearts, plan work schedules accounting only for what the mind says and leaving out what the body is telling us, target how results affect "us" and don't take "them" into account, we are forgetting that everything is connected. Embodied Leaders embrace the reality that the head and the heart, the mind and the body, the perspectives of us and them can and should be integrated for healthy leadership to happen.

Developing Felt Sense

In the words of Deb Dana, a therapist and author who has translated research on the autonomic nervous system and brought it into practice, "Story follows state." But what does this mean exactly?

When you are living an experience, sensations related to that experience will show up as body sensations first, creating a state, or way of being. Then your thinking mind will come up with a story. For instance, if your body feels cold and your mind brings awareness to your body, it will interpret, or make up a story, that you need to do something to get warm. You might grab a sweater. Your body will then make the necessary shifts to change your state.

In Pillar 1, we referred to your body as a "somatic co-pilot," and for good reason. The body often notices before the mind. As early as the 1890s, psychologist William James proposed that emotion follows physiological changes that are experienced in the body and communicated to the brain via the nervous system. The body acts before the mind becomes aware.

More recent mind-body-based psychotherapies are furthering our understanding, even connecting where we physically look with our eyes to releasing unprocessed trauma.

Thoughts, feelings, and physical sensations all involve interpretations in the brain. We often attribute more importance to sensations that we understand as thoughts than to sensations that we understand as physical. When we overemphasize thoughts, we miss out on the opportunity to tap into our body in order to direct the course of our life.

For instance, at the start of Andrew's embodiment journey, when he described his insomnia, he talked about his thoughts, and how he was ruminating about the same things over and over again. It took some probing to get him to reflect on what was happening in his body—how the pace of his breath was fast, how his muscles were holding tension, how he kept tossing and turning as his mind went around in circles. By noticing and acknowledging the importance of those physical sensations and manifestations, Andrew was able to find practices that would improve his sleep, like breathing and body-scanning practices.

What about you? What would it be like to give more power to the sensations that you feel, versus thoughts? How would bringing your body on board in this way influence your decision-making and actions?

About 80 percent of the information passing between your body and your brain goes from your body to your brain.

Developing felt sense is a way to tap into your body's voice, knowledge, and wisdom. When you bring awareness to thoughts, feelings, memories, and physical sensations, and experience them directly before the mind starts to build stories around them, you are experiencing felt sense. If you listen, your body will give you the information you need to make better decisions.

For instance, consider a typical work situation where someone asks you to take on another project. Do you pause and check in with your body before answering? If you do, you may find that you respond more wisely. A feeling of constriction or panic in the body likely suggests that you need more information or an adjustment to your current commitments to make saying yes to this additional project workable. A feeling of expansion, openness, or excitement in the body may suggest that this project is exactly what you need right now.

Your body is constantly sending you this type of information. About 80 percent of the information passing between your body and your brain goes in the *afferent* direction—the pathway from your body to your brain. It is up to you to make use of this vast amount of information in a way that is ultimately helpful. In her book *Whole Brain Living*, neuroanatomist and author Jill Bolte Taylor describes the nature of humans as "feeling creatures who think, rather than thinking creatures who feel." Bolte Taylor writes that "any attempt we may make to bypass or ignore what we are feeling may have the power to derail our mental health."

Understanding Your Nervous System

Our goal here is to give you just enough understanding of what is going on inside you to allow you to strategically apply your attention to what matters most. This includes how body sensations and feelings arise, how you react to others and yourself, and how you relate with your own self-talk. It also involves bringing awareness to patterns of behavior that are serving you and to those that are no longer beneficial. Through *self-awareness*, you can tap your own mind-body information flow to improve your life and leadership.

So let's start with a quick primer on the nervous system.

Your nervous system is a highly sophisticated information network. It gathers data from both inside and outside your body, and transmits these data to and from all parts of your body. It includes large nerves that connect your heart, lungs, and digestive tract to your brain, as well as smaller nerves that extend to the tips of your fingers and toes.

The central nervous system

Your brain sits at the very top of this information network and, with your spinal cord, forms what is called the central nervous system.

The central nervous system controls most of your bodily and mental processes. It is responsible for seeing, breathing, moving, feeling physical sensations, thinking, and more. At a very high level, your brain is composed of three main parts: the cerebrum, the brain stem, and the cerebellum. Your spinal cord extends from the bottom of the brain stem, at the medulla. (See diagram on the opposite page.)

Your cerebrum contains your cerebral cortex, or the gray matter—the outermost layer—of your brain. At the front of your frontal lobe is your prefrontal cortex, which is responsible for planning and anticipating, regulating emotions (such as stopping inappropriate actions), and empathetic understanding. It is the part of your brain that goes "offline" when under high stress.

Closely linked to your prefrontal cortex is the limbic system. The limbic system controls the stress response and supports many functions related to memory, emotions, and behavior. It maintains survival by adapting to the environment.

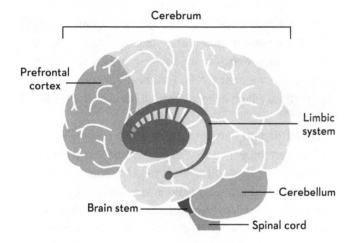

Cerebrum

Prefrontal cortex

Limbic system

Cerebellum

Brain stem

Spinal cord

Your cerebellum is found behind the brain stem and is responsible for movement, balance, and posture.

The brain stem, or your primitive brain, is responsible for regulating heart rate, breathing, hunger, sleep, and other basic physiological functions.

The peripheral nervous system

The peripheral nervous system is composed of the nerves that are outside your brain and spinal cord. While the central nervous system can be seen as a central hub, the peripheral nervous system allows you to get more precise "on-the-ground" data and undertake more nuanced actions. The peripheral nervous system speaks directly to your muscles, gathers up and transmits sensory information about what is going on inside and outside you, and is responsible for your body's automatic functions, such as the beating of your heart, digestion, and sweating.

This automatic part of the peripheral nervous system is called the autonomic nervous system. It is further divided into the sympathetic nervous system, which stimulates a response to danger or stress, and the parasympathetic nervous system, which governs rest, digestion, and repair of the body.

The autonomic nervous system also contains the enteric nervous system, which controls gastrointestinal behavior. Because of the large number of neurons that it contains, and its ability to act locally and independently, the enteric nervous system is also sometimes called our "second brain." This gut-level neurology plays a role in our lived experience, giving us "gut feelings."

Systems out of balance

When your central and peripheral nervous systems are integrated and working in harmony, you feel good, you sleep well, your mind is sharp, and you feel in control. When the systems go out of balance, because of stress, trauma, or illness, you feel off, your sleep is poor, your memory and cognitive functions are not as strong, and/or you feel out of control. Patterns deeply programmed into your mind-body often take over automatically, as a way to efficiently deal with the imbalance.

For instance, Andrew shared that when he is under pressure, or when things aren't going as planned at work, his old pattern of bursting into anger can overtake him. His prefrontal cortex goes offline, he loses the ability to rationally choose his reactions, he lashes out, and he regrets it later once his system calms down. You probably have your own patterns for responding to stress.

Polyvagal theory (explored below) can help you understand your nervous system and its response to your internal and external worlds, including when you're stressed.

Stress and Burnout

The stress response is adaptive and biologically driven. It is meant to protect. Your mind-body is smart, and it is constantly reading internal and external environmental signals to adjust so that you stay safe. When you are stressed, your nervous system shifts from focusing on social engagement to survival mode, and thus your prefrontal cortex goes offline.

In addition, when your mind-body perceives a threat, it releases hormones, including adrenaline and cortisol, that increase your heart rate, your blood pressure, and the glucose in your bloodstream so that you have a ready source of energy to act.

The energy that is made available during short-term stress is meant to be used up fairly quickly. In times when humans lived as hunters and gatherers, this energy would be used to run away from a threat in order to survive.

When your day is filled with chronic stressors, it is difficult for your body to use up that energy or to know when to turn off the stress response system. As a result, stress hormones and excess glucose are ever-present, causing inflammation and dysregulation that can lead to numerous health problems. This includes burnout, which leaders around the world are currently experiencing at record levels. Burnout, which is different from depression, consists of emotional exhaustion, decreased sense of accomplishment, and a feeling of disconnection from oneself. In essence, burnout is an experience of disembodiment.

After a prolonged period of high levels of stress in his fast-paced, high-pressure environment, Andrew experienced the symptoms of burnout. "I just didn't feel like myself. I couldn't escape the lows, I never felt rested, and I lost my motivation to do anything, which was so frustrating because I was used to being a high-functioning achiever," Andrew shared. "Thank God for my property out in the trees! I went there as often as I could, and I think it helped me come back quicker than if I wasn't able to spend so much time in nature."

When Casey was preparing to share her TEDx Talk, "Let Your Body Lead," she experienced way more stress than she anticipated. "I love public speaking and was so grateful for the opportunity to share a message about embodiment that I felt to be so important, but the process really challenged so many elements of what I thought I knew to be true," she confided. "In addition, I'd never spoken in front of more than a thousand people before, and I'd put a lot of pressure on myself to make it amazing. I worked myself into a frenzy.

The energy required for such a creation also pulled me away from my business and added some elements of financial stress I wasn't expecting." Ironically, she wasn't practicing what she preached in various parts of the process, and her body felt it. She began to experience aches and pains, anxiety that was previously unfamiliar to her, and insomnia. Casey added: "These symptoms contributed to the overall contraction and heaviness I felt in my body. I knew my body was asking for a break, but it was hard to listen, because I was scared that if I took a break, I wouldn't get my talk done in time, I'd have nothing good to say, and I'd make a fool of myself in front of a whole bunch of people!"

Have you ever felt that inner resistance? Have you experienced the voice that says you just need to keep pushing through, even when what you're doing is not really working?

Eventually, Casey recognized the irony in how she was acting: "I was creating a talk about letting the body lead, while my mental stories were running the show!" She knew she had to put her body back in the driver's seat. She refocused on meditation, breathwork practices, bike rides, rest, recovery, and play. She even decided to prioritize massages to help her process the stress and calm her nervous system. "This way of adapting in alignment with my body's needs really helped in the weeks leading up to being on that stage. And—go figure—it made creating the talk so much easier. In fact, I received one-liners in meditation, visions connected to the talk in breathwork, ideas on bike rides, and truths about what I wanted to say while resting, recovering, and playing!"

Now, what about you? Can you think of a recent situation where you felt stressed? What did it feel like in your body? You may have felt emotions such as anxiety or nervousness, which we might refer to as "flight" energy. Or you may have felt emotions like anger or irritability, which could be referred to as "fight" energy. Or you may have felt nothing, as though your emotions were completely numbed, which we could call "shutdown" energy.

To what extent did your physiological response serve you in that situation, and how quickly were you able to return to a calm and socially engaged state?

Regulating your stress response is crucial to your well-being, and to the well-being of those around you. It will help you reduce reactivity and unhealthy relationship dynamics, and safeguard you against burnout. Key to regulating your nervous system is carving out some time that is restful and not focused on doing, every day. As an Embodied Leader, you become aware of the story you tell yourself around stress, and where you might get stuck. Polyvagal theory helps you understand and bring awareness to the story—to your interpretation of your stress response.

Polyvagal Theory

Polyvagal theory, developed by Stephen Porges, has been described as an "embodiment" theory. It proposes three hierarchical states that run along a continuum, from a calm and socially engaged state to an immobilized, shutdown state.

Within the parasympathetic nervous system, we find two pathways—ventral and dorsal—which run along an important nerve called the vagus nerve. The ventral pathway creates a calm and socially engaged state. The dorsal pathway brings about the shutdown or immobilized stress state.

The vagus nerve is the tenth and longest cranial nerve, running from the brain to the lower abdomen and interfacing with the heart, lungs, liver, and digestive tract. The vagus nerve has a role in almost everything we do. It even boosts oxytocin—the feel-good love hormone. The vagus nerve is taking center stage these days thanks to the role it plays in regulating the immune system. It may also act as a potential "off switch" for numerous diseases and conditions, including depression and anxiety, epilepsy, rheumatoid arthritis, and inflammatory bowel disease.

The strength of your vagus nerve is referred to as your "vagal control," a key physiological marker of your vulnerability to stress. High vagal control is your ability to quickly go from a stressed to a calm state; it is associated with better thinking, emotion regulation, empathy, and improved social connections. Low vagal control, which is the result of a hyperactive stress response, is associated with greater levels of anxiety, anger, and stress hormones like cortisol. If you are anything like us, you will appreciate more vagal control.

The autonomic ladder

The autonomic ladder, as described by Deb Dana, is a useful way to understand how we experience polyvagal theory.

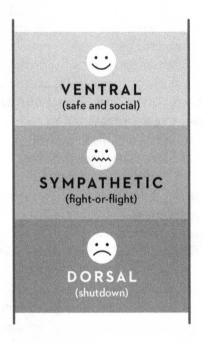

VENTRAL
(safe and social)

SYMPATHETIC
(fight-or-flight)

DORSAL
(shutdown)

At the top of the ladder is your "safe and social" state, or the ventral state in polyvagal theory. You are relaxed and socially engaged when in this state. You feel calm and present, and if you were a river, you would be flowing with soft waves. This state is your "home" state, and you are best served when spending the majority of your time here. You are likely in this state when working on a favorite task and/or connecting with a colleague or loved one in a relaxed moment. When Andrew is sipping his coffee with his wife before heading into work in the morning, or when he is in his meditation practice, he is in his safe and social state.

A step down on the ladder is your mobilized state—one of fight-or-flight, sympathetic nervous system arousal, or panic. This is the state you might experience when faced with a threat or other type of stressor. For instance, you start your workday and get an email with an urgent request. Your schedule is already packed, and you begin to sweat. In this hyper-aroused state, your sympathetic nervous system kicks in to protect you, even if the threat is relatively benign. You feel tense and overwhelmed and now the river is flowing faster and with bigger, choppy waves. Even now, Andrew occasionally experiences his mobilized state in high-pressure meetings, and it can lead him to angry outbursts.

At the bottom of the ladder is your dorsal state, which is characterized by immobilization and shutdown. In this hypo-aroused state, you might feel numb, tapped out, or not engaged at all. Your river has stopped flowing. When stressed, some people travel very quickly down the ladder to this shutdown state. Andrew noted that when a combination of stressors "come at him" all at once, he finds himself moving down the ladder. The big meeting, combined with skipping lunch, combined with learning that his daughter had an incident at school, eventually land him in a shutdown state, where he has no bandwidth for social engagement. He checks out with a glass of bourbon and the game.

Both the sympathetic (fight-or-flight) and dorsal (shutdown) states are stress states, but they look and feel quite different, and require different strategies to bring you back to a safe and social state.

Which of the three states are you in right now?

If you are feeling low energy, depressed, hopeless, or numb, you are likely at the bottom of the ladder, in a shutdown or dorsal state.

If you are feeling a flood of energy, agitation, stress, or irritability, you are likely midway up the ladder, in a sympathetic or mobilized state (fight-or-flight).

If you are feeling calm, secure, socially engaged, or playful, you are likely at the top of the ladder, in a safe and social or ventral state.

If your home state is safe and social, you likely have a go-to state when under stress, or your "home away from home." What is it for you?

Julie's home away from home is the sympathetic state. It shows up for her as irritability and a sense of pressure. "I start moving faster, making mistakes—bumping into or dropping things—lose my appetite, and feel more restless," she remarked. Having this as her home away from home is one of the reasons exercise has been a lifelong strategy for her, as it helps her release stress energy from her body. For this reason, Julie has such gratitude for her movement practices. In fact, many people find that movement is the quickest and most effective way of releasing this type of energy. Can you relate?

Self-Mastery and Resilience

Mastering your nervous system's response to what is going on inside and outside you starts with awareness. The patterns of your autonomic nervous system are biologically driven and developed through experience. How you respond to a stressful situation is learned, and adaptive in the moment. *You do not choose your stress response.* The good news is that you do not need to waste energy trying to get rid of old patterns. You can instead learn to notice the patterns and, with compassion, bring explicit awareness to choosing how you respond. By slowing down the process and with awareness, you can grow and embody new patterns of more helpful responses given each circumstance.

> The head and the heart,
> the mind and the body,
> **the perspectives of us and**
> **them can be integrated.**

It is wise to notice what it feels like to be in the ventral state (safe and social), and notice when you fall out of that state into the sympathetic state (fight-or-flight) or the dorsal state (shutdown). What do each of these states feel like in your own body? Under what circumstances are you most likely to experience them? When are you most likely to move down the ladder, from ventral to sympathetic to dorsal?

When you notice that you are out of the ventral state, the key is to learn how to move up the ladder, back to safe and social. The goal is not to be in a ventral state all the time, but to learn how to return to it quickly when you notice that you are in a state of stress. You may also be in a mixed state that allows you to have both a sense of safety and either stillness—such as while sleeping or in self-reflection, which is a mix of dorsal and ventral—or playfulness, which is mixed sympathetic and ventral.

Sometimes you may need to protect yourself from the outside world. Remember, though, that putting on your armor locks energy and emotions inside you that eventually will need to be released. Armoring up can also keep positive energy out. For instance, you may deflect a compliment because you feel embarrassed or unworthy, instead of receiving and acknowledging it.

Your Window of Resilience

We all have different thresholds for stress. The more tolerance we have for stressors and demands, the better we are able to respond in productive ways and to stay in a ventral vagal state. You can think of this as your "window of tolerance," as defined by Daniel Siegel, or your "window of resilience," which is the term that we prefer. When you are in your window of resilience, you feel safe and secure, and no alarms are going off. You are neither overaroused nor underaroused.

To get a feel for this optimal, embodied state, consider a scale from 1 to 10, with 10 being overwhelmed or distressed. We all know that feeling of being overwhelmed, whether it be related to feelings of stress, sadness, anger, or any other emotion. When in a state of 7 or higher on this scale, you are outside your window of resilience, and your prefrontal cortex goes offline. Your ability to regulate emotions, make decisions, focus, or problem-solve is severely affected when in this state. This is the "don't even try to have a conversation with your business partner" state!

When in a state of 3 or lower, you are hypo-aroused (understimulated). You feel lethargic, unmotivated, withdrawn, or shutdown.

Optimal functioning is when you are below 7 and above 3 out of 10. Here you are better able to think logically, be emotionally attuned, engage socially, and respond to life rather than react.

This range is your window of resilience.

In different people, the lines at which they cross over into hyper- or hypo-stimulation are quite far from each other, meaning they have a wide window of resilience. In others, the lines are much closer, implying a small window of resilience, which can be experienced as very high reactivity and difficulty staying in a calm, attuned, engaged state.

Your window is not fixed. Because your mind-body is changeable, you can reshape and rewire your neural pathways. You have the power not only to return to your window of resilience but also to grow a wider space in which you can experience optimal functioning and lead with your whole self. Through awareness and practice, you develop a level of mastery that leads to greater feelings of safety and security in your system. And when you feel safe and secure, you are more resilient, and better able to handle the stressors of life and leadership.

So how do you inhabit and grow your window of resilience?

The key is being able to pause and become present before responding. To do this, you need to be aware of what is happening inside you in the present moment. You need to slow down to feel what is going on in your body, and notice your level of stimulation or arousal. Pausing gives you the opportunity to tune in to, and connect to, your body. According to Master Somatic Leadership Coach Amanda Blake, presence requires us to pay attention to the sensations we are feeling right now: "Your ability to observe your own sensations without immediately reacting to them is precisely what makes presence possible." Both pausing and allowing yourself to notice the sensations of your body are key.

What helps you to pause and become present? How do you come back to the present moment?

Whatever connects you to the present, to being rather than doing, will help you tune in to your body and to the present moment.

In the present, you can respond with what you need. When you find yourself in a hypo-stimulated state, you can use your body to bring yourself back to your window of resilience. For example, you might shift your body posture to a more engaged position, engage in some gentle movement (standing up, walking, stretching), or connect to your surroundings (feel your feet or body supported beneath you; notice three things in your environment). As you make these shifts, you will come into a more stimulated state; this is the natural progression of stress. When you find yourself in a hyper-stimulated state, you can use more vigorous movement of any sort and more dynamic breathing exercises to bring yourself back. The exercises at the end of this pillar will help you to build your competence at coming back to your window of resilience.

Strengthening and transmitting resilience

When you are in your window of resilience, others will notice. They will also notice when you are stressed or bored. This awareness may be conscious or unconscious, such as the body noticing and responding differently without conscious awareness of doing so.

When Andrew is in his window of resilience, he really is "Zen-like," and operates in the Integrator style. He feels calm, people around him feel calm, and he facilitates real connection and creative conversations among his team, even when there is a lot going on. He says, "It's as if I'm accessing ALL of my wisdom."

When your body is on board in this optimal state, you have more complete access to your senses and your emotions, and can see the big picture. You are more likely to embody the Integrator style. You are able to access the ventral vagal state that allows you to connect authentically with others. You send a signal to those around you that you are safe to be around, open to connecting, and available for authentic engagement.

In a leadership context, helping others feel safe in your presence allows them to take risks, practice courage, and innovate. There's more on this in Pillar 3. When you maintain an optimal state, you help others to move into and grow their own window of resilience. This is co-regulation at its best, as described in more detail in Pillar 4.

When you are outside your window of resilience, you cannot tap into your personal resources to give clear direction or guidance, to solve problems, or to listen with compassion. You send a signal to those around you that it may not be safe to share ideas or connect authentically. That signal causes others to play it safe and put up protective barriers when they are around you. If people in a group find themselves outside their window of resilience, it affects the resilience of the entire group.

Andrew practiced and learned to master his autonomic ladder. He could then be more effective in his team meetings. Now, when he feels his system becoming hyper-aroused in those meetings, his go-to technique is to repeatedly take two inhales through the nose and one exhale through the mouth—what is known as a physiological sigh. This helps him stay in or return to his safe and social state.

Resilience is a virtuous cycle. The more resilient you and others around you are, the more resilience will grow. As mentioned above, to inhabit and grow your window of resilience, you need to pause and bring awareness to the state you are in. You can also grow your window of resilience by strengthening your vagal response through specific exercises, some of which are described below. As you grow your window of resilience, fewer stressors will push you into hyper- or hypo-arousal, and you will spend less time in these stress states.

Exercises to Bring Your Body on Board

Notice your body's signals

Choose a trusted partner or friend to share with, or you can journal about your experience. Share something positive that has happened in your day, and pay particular attention to anything that you notice in your body as you share your story.

You may feel warmth, openness, tension, tingling, sadness, or any other emotion or feeling. At first, you may not notice anything, and that is okay too. Describe what you are noticing in as much detail as you can.

Now, share something difficult that has happened in your day, and pay attention to the sensations in your body as you share your story. Notice how they are similar to or different from when you shared the positive story. Describe what you are noticing in as much detail as you can.

Bring this new awareness into your day-to-day, paying attention to your body's signals in response to different situations.

Master the autonomic ladder

Tap into your ability to find where you are on the ladder and what state you are in.

If you are at the bottom of the ladder, in a shutdown or dorsal state, how can you change your state to feel more connected and safe? You might find it helpful to bring gentle, intentional movement into your body by going for a slow walk or stretching. You may also benefit from connecting to your five senses to bring you back to the present moment, noticing the sounds, sights, smells, and so on around you.

If you are midway, in a sympathetic or mobilized state (fight-or-flight), how can you change your state to feel more grounded and calm? You likely need to discharge the fight-or-flight energy with some more vigorous movement: shake out your limbs, do some jumping jacks or push-ups, or dance freely. Alternatively, you might actively engage with someone by taking a walk with or phoning a friend and having a little rant, or you could listen to music or a podcast that matches the energy you are feeling. Taking one to two physiological sighs may also be helpful: double inhale through the nose, single exhale through the mouth.

The more you practice helping yourself move up the ladder, the more you will master the skill of changing your state and feeling secure, safe, and connected more of the time.

Widen your window of resilience

Think about a moment when you were right in the middle of your window of resilience, when you felt grounded, content, and present.

Now imagine a time when you were pulled out of this balanced state, into hyper-arousal. Bring as much detail to mind as you can. What did it feel like in your body then? What does it feel like now when you recall it? Come back to the present moment by engaging with your senses—grounding your feet, touching an object near you, taking a breath, or engaging in another sensory experience that works for you.

Now imagine a time when you were pulled into hypo-arousal. What did it feel like in your body then? What does it feel like now when you recall it? Come back to the present moment by engaging with your senses again.

By exploring the edges of your window of resilience, you build up your tolerance for discomfort and increase your ability to stay regulated or quickly come back to a regulated state when faced with stress or other triggers.

Taking Risks and Practicing Courage

Growth depends
on your ability to step out
of your comfort zone,
be with discomfort, and
navigate fear courageously.

MELISSA, A JOURNALIST turned body-positive activist, entrepreneur, and influencer with a huge following, shared that she used to be a performer as a child. "I was so embodied!" she exclaimed. "I was into theater, expressed myself openly, and was vibrant and full of life. Back then, I felt the fear, and did it anyway," she said with a reflective look on her face, almost in awe of her inner child. Melissa, like a lot of us, experienced many qualities of the Integrator as a kid.

She continued: "Then, in my twenties, I started dieting and became so disconnected from my body, my truth, and my courage. For a decade, I completely lost that natural, embodied way of living. I struggled with an eating disorder; I barely slept, and didn't listen to my body's most natural cues. Being a journalist didn't help. I sacrificed my body in whatever way I felt I needed to, to cover a story. I completely forgot what living in an embodied way was actually like." Melissa resonated more with the Explorer throughout this season.

"Shit hit the fan with my eating disorder, and it led to me starting therapy," she said. "My therapist used somatic techniques in her practice, and would often ask me questions about what was happening in my body. It was hard to answer those questions at first, but slowly, over time,

I became more connected. Stumbling upon the book *Intuitive Eating* helped too. It offered a whole new way of being around food. Even though it was scary, I learned how to trust my body again to help me decide how to eat. My eating disorder was a gateway to disembodiment, and intuitive eating coupled with somatic therapy offered a gateway back home." She embodied the Connector as she continued to heal.

For Melissa, embodiment didn't just change her relationship with food, it changed everything, including her career. She went back to school to become a dietitian, then integrated her communication skills and personal experience with her new professional credentials to help others in their relationships with food and their bodies. She has expanded her reach through podcasting and speaking.

The conversation came full circle when Melissa, as Integrator, stated: "I've reclaimed that childhood power and courage, especially as I've become more visible. I don't self-silence like I used to." Melissa learned how to be with fear—especially when she's about to speak to a large audience. "My heart races faster, my palms sweat, and I feel heat in my body—that's the fear. And then I use my tools. I breathe deeper, I feel the ground beneath my feet, and I allow this sense of peace to flow through me, so that I can share my voice, even when I'm scared."

As a leader, it's likely that you have experience with navigating fear. That could be when speaking to a large audience, as Melissa did; when navigating a difficult cash-flow issue as a business owner; when contemplating a tragic thought as a parent after reveling in your child's sweet innocence; or in any number of situations.

Fear is part of the human experience, and yet we are universally wired to avoid it—and the associated discomfort that shows up in the body—in order to feel safe and secure. But growth depends on your ability to step out of your comfort zone, be with discomfort, and navigate fear courageously. By taking risks and practicing courage, you strengthen your ability to adapt to future stress and build the resilience needed to move into new life and leadership experiences. Consider the wise words of psychiatrist Fritz Perls: "Fear is excitement without the breath."

This pillar is about the courage required to belong to yourself, and to return to your body when faced with especially difficult situations and sensations. You will understand why taking risks and practicing courage is key to being an Embodied Leader. You will also learn how to feel the fear in your body and "do it anyway," building the resilience you need to live and lead to your fullest potential.

Being with Discomfort

What do taking risks and practicing courage have to do with embodied leadership?

Let's break it down.

In the process of embodiment, you learn to feel sensations in your body and to excavate those sensations for wisdom, so that you can receive guidance for your life. Courage helps you to go there—to enter into and explore the vast and often unknown territory of your body's wisdom, with the potential to feel what may be uncomfortable or even painful. Even allowing yourself to feel positive sensations inside your body can be challenging if you are not used to them. It takes courage to stay with the sensations long enough to receive wisdom from them, and then to act thoughtfully based on that wisdom. There will be more on trusting and integrating your body's wisdom in Pillar 5.

In Pillar 2, you learned about the roles the mind-body and nervous system play in consciously processing your day-to-day experiences. You learned that engaging in practices to widen your window of resilience can help you live and lead from your safe-and-social ventral vagal state, and how you can be in this state more often.

But you don't simply widen your window of resilience overnight. You do it incrementally by courageously and consciously attuning to uncomfortable sensations in your body, without being overtaken by them. You stretch your capacity to handle challenging moments because "all growth starts at the end of your comfort zone." Through this growth, you become more responsive, rather than reactive, and you develop an adaptive relationship with stress that allows you to build resilience and better respond to future stressors. Not only do you bring your body on board as a somatic co-pilot, but you keep it on board for navigating what's to come.

Each time Melissa notices her heart racing and palms sweating before presenting to a large group of people, and each time she chooses to attune to her breath, ground through her feet, and be with the uncomfortable sensations without letting them overtake her, her window of resilience increases. Speaking in front of large groups gets easier because she trains her nervous system to stay in or return more quickly to a safe and social state, even under pressure.

In leadership, courage is required to move through many vulnerable moments. Embodied Leaders have hard conversations, set boundaries, and set themselves up with the potential to be rejected. This is how they facilitate growth, for themselves, for others, and for the collective whole. Embodied Leaders hold space for differing opinions, act as allies, and are responsible for effectively resolving conflict. They move from a place of gripping for control and micromanaging to one of trusting, empowering, and collaborating with others.

Vulnerability Is Courage

As you have likely experienced, vulnerability is something you can feel in your body, and you may rate that sensation as being anywhere from mildly uncomfortable to deeply distressing. Vulnerability can be sensed as a contraction or constriction in your body, such as a knot in your stomach, a racing sensation in your heart space, or a tension in your neck and shoulders. Regardless of what you feel and where you feel it, vulnerability doesn't feel good on the surface, and without awareness and practice of being with those sensations, it can be easier to run away from vulnerability and the associated discomfort. Researcher and best-selling author Brené Brown has given us all a lot to think about when it comes to vulnerability. In her powerful TED Talk on the subject, she reminds us that: (1) we cannot selectively numb emotions, and that includes vulnerability; (2) vulnerability is the birthplace of joy, creativity, belonging, and love; and (3) vulnerability takes courage and involves risk. For connection to happen, we have to allow ourselves to be seen. If you run away from vulnerability, you risk losing connection—with others and with yourself. So it is important to question why you are running, and what you are afraid of.

_____

If you run away from vulnerability, you risk losing connection—with others and with yourself. **Why are you running, and what are you afraid of?**

_____

Embodied leadership invites you to bring awareness to vulnerability and to all uncomfortable sensations. Through this work, you will elevate your capacity to "be with" discomfort, and to choose what to do next from a place of conscious responsiveness rather than nonconscious reactivity.

In April 2020, Casey had been working closely with a new team member in her business for a few months. She hired this team member to support the company's marketing initiatives. Casey shared: "Though things had been going relatively well, I noticed myself becoming more and more dysregulated or 'triggered' by interactions with them and marketing choices they were making, even though they were a very competent marketer. Old patterns were arising in me that created tension in my body and made me want to grip for control, micromanage, and fix the things I per-ceived them to be doing wrong."

Casey eventually realized that she was feeling over-whelmed—which she experienced as energy swirling above her head and difficulty dropping into her body and the pres-ent moment. "I didn't know what was happening for me as a business owner with the start of a looming pandemic. The stress of the time made my nervous system want to fight, and then shut down."

When she realized this, Casey understood that even though it was hard to ask for, what she really needed was more support, not less. Taking back control, isolating, and micromanaging were part of an old "comfortable" pattern that would sabotage her success and growth. "What I really needed was more courage," Casey commented. "I needed the courage to share my vulnerability as a business owner, to communicate what I was feeling uncomfortable about, to risk being rejected, and to trust that we could come up with solutions together." Feeling the fear in her body and "doing it anyways," Casey reached out to her team member and openly communicated with them about how she was feeling. The team member, in turn, shared honestly about what had been coming up for them, and they worked it out, together.

When you practice courage, you choose to pay atten-tion to what you are feeling, even when it's uncomfortable. When you pay attention to what you are feeling, you get insight into what you need as a leader. Courage will help you to hold space for yourself, your needs, and your desires, and it will also help you to be open and receptive to others. When you know what you need and desire, it is easier to communicate and work together to get them met. This leads to more meaningful connections among people on a team and, therefore, more optimal teamwork. In Pillar 4, you'll explore connecting with yourself and others in more depth.

By being courageous, you inspire courage in others and contribute to the co-creation of greater inner fulfillment and more aligned success, no matter where you lead.

Risks and Rewards

Nobel Prize–winning poet T.S. Eliot said that "only those who will risk going too far can possibly find out how far they can go."

Whether you are leading a team, a business, or yourself, part of your ability to create and innovate in the face of challenges depends on your willingness to take risks.

At its most basic level, risk is about uncertainty. It is about the likelihood that a future event will occur, and the impact that future event may have. Risk is connected to fear, in that how you perceive and feel about uncertainty can have a direct impact on your nervous system, which, as we discussed in Pillar 2, will influence the degree to which you can be intentional in your actions. When you are fearful, you may overestimate risk and be unduly biased in how you evaluate information. This can make decision-making and finding the courage to act more difficult.

Risk tolerance and risk appetite are generally defined in business or financial terms. Risk tolerance is the degree of risk or uncertainty that is acceptable to you. Risk appetite is the amount of risk you are willing to take on to achieve your goals, before taking actions to mitigate the risk.

In the case of Melissa, working as a body-positive activist requires a high level of risk tolerance, as there can be much uncertainty and potential volatility in this space. When Melissa feels fear before speaking in front of a crowd and speaks anyway, that reflects her risk appetite—she is willing to take on the potential reactions, criticisms, rejection, and so on, because her broader goal makes it worth it.

While risk, risk tolerance, and risk appetite are well understood from a business perspective, they are rarely discussed from the perspective of the mind-body.

- Based on what you have learned so far, how might your place on the autonomic ladder affect your willingness to take on risk?

- Do people with a wider window of resilience tend to be more comfortable with risk or less?

- How might greater levels of embodiment increase your comfort with risk, and how might this serve you?

Ever since psychologists Dana Carney, Amy Cuddy, and Andy Yap reported that posing in high-power nonverbal displays increased feelings of power and risk tolerance in both men and women, there has been significant debate about such "power poses." At the same time, human physiology studies have shown that holding more expansive postures can increase testosterone and decrease cortisol in the bloodstream. Whether your body is in a contractive position (arms crossed, legs crossed, folded in) or an expansive pose (open chest, arms wide, legs wide and grounded), your physical stance may influence your state of being, and that feeling of power may make you more comfortable with taking on risk. What do you think? We invite you to try out different poses for yourself. What do you notice? In what position do you feel more ready to engage with the world?

For quite some time, Courtney has used expansive body postures before going into meetings or engaging in difficult conversations. She spoke openly about it in the office, and although many colleagues found it amusing to see her standing outside a meeting room looking like a starfish, a few started to adopt the behavior. Allowing herself to be vulnerable, Courtney shared, "As someone who manages generalized anxiety, I can say with the confidence of experimenting on myself that expansive postures reduce my anxiety, nervousness, and fear, and they give me the boost I need to walk into that room and give that presentation." When Courtney shows up calm and present, empowered and embodied, the people around her sense that, and their nervous systems have the opportunity to join her in that space. We will talk more about this shared space, or co-regulation, in Pillar 4.

In today's complex and fast-paced world, taking risks and learning from both successes and failures are absolute necessities. We can't grow a business without taking risks. We can't build trust with people around us without taking risks. We take risks whenever we invest money, time, and emotional effort in a new venture. We take risks when we are vulnerable. There is no reward without risk.

Embodied leadership helps you grow the resilience and presence needed to assess and act on risk in the most generative way possible, to achieve your highest goals. And if you surround yourself with others who share your vision and are inspired to act because they feel safe, secure, and connected, you can accomplish incredible things together.

Where You Might Get Stuck

To be human means to have basic requirements that we are strongly motivated to satisfy. You are likely familiar with Maslow's hierarchy and the fact that we are driven to meet our fundamental needs first, before we can be concerned with growth and self-actualization. Your nervous system is designed to prioritize your fundamental needs, which include your physiological needs, your need for safety and security, your need for love and belonging, and your need for esteem and self-worth. And because these needs are the priority, it is very common to engage in behaviors such as molding and adapting yourself to fit in, allowing your boundaries to be crossed to get your social needs met, or going into autopilot to navigate an emotionally charged situation.

During your introspective journey toward greater authenticity, alignment, and embodiment, autopilot mode may feel less and less comfortable. When engaging in activities that are not aligned with your values, you may start to notice a reaction or tension in your body. Your body will ask you to have the courage to choose change. Breaking out of autopilot can feel risky. Being true to yourself can feel as if your sense of belonging and even your physical safety are at stake, because sometimes they are. Rocking the boat may feel very scary, but cognitive psychologist and author Scott Barry Kaufman argues that finding purpose and fulfillment requires us to take these risks, to propel our own growth. Kaufman builds on Maslow's work and proposes a sailboat metaphor to depict how our need for security (self-esteem, connection, and safety: the body of the boat) must work in dynamic integration with our need to grow (purpose, love, and exploration: the sails of the boat) to propel us to our highest potential.

If you surround yourself with others who are inspired to act because they feel safe, secure, and connected, you can accomplish incredible things together.

Julie has been told that she does many things differently. She explained: "I squat as I wait in line at the grocery store and sometimes in meetings too. I have been known to check my bike with a concierge service before a fancy gala when there is nowhere to lock my bike outside, because I choose active transport most of the time. I don't have chairs in my home; I have stools and floor cushions."

Julie recognizes that the choices she makes are outside the norm. For many years she attempted to fly "under the radar" and hide her authentic behaviors. She didn't want extra attention or to receive negative judgments from others. Certainly, she received implicit and explicit messages from others that it would be better to behave more like them; but for her, not showing up fully across the different areas of her life took so much extra energy. Living more in alignment by owning her way of doing things, without justifying or apologizing, has meant taking risks that are totally worth it. "When I live in alignment with my values and desired behaviors, I feel liberated and empowered, even if others don't understand," she added.

Standing alone can be scary for anyone, but especially for people who have experienced systemic oppression. If you live in a woman's body, a trans body, a fat body, a disabled body, a body of color, and/or a neurodiverse body, there can be even more risk involved with being authentically who you are. More work must be done collectively to create safety for people with different identities, and extra courage may be required for people to reprogram internalized belief systems about being less than what's considered the norm. As an Embodied Leader, regardless of your circumstances, how are you using whatever privilege you have to create safe spaces and opportunities for everyone, and to what extent do you feel comfortable acting as an ally? These are big, important questions for our times, and making progress in these areas requires courage. There are many excellent resources available to help you go deeper with these questions, including Resmaa Menakem's *My*

Grandmother's Hands, Bärí A. Williams's *Diversity in the Workplace,* and Ruchika Tulshyan's *Inclusion on Purpose.* We cannot do justice to these important topics in this book, but many other authors, leaders, and experts have done so. We encourage you to explore these topics further and, as a leader, to ensure that the foundations for thoughtful policies, practices, and actions regarding diversity, equity, and inclusion are in place. Leaders must truly act with integrity to build stronger and more cohesive communities and organizations.

Your Body Has Your Back

Julie recalls walking along a corridor to attend a meeting with her two bosses—a psychology leader and a program leader within the hospital setting where she was working. "I was aware of ongoing budget cuts and had already experienced a significant change because of them," she began. "I had a sinking feeling in my stomach that this meeting was to bring me news that my position had been impacted." She was correct. As the news landed, she noticed an initial feeling of overwhelm. She then brought her attention to her breath, and with mindful awareness directed her attention to the place in her body where she felt most grounded: her feet. "I began to gently rock my feet back and forth in my shoes, and grounded my body. I noticed the sense of overwhelm soften and was able to be more present in the meeting and plan next steps, with compassion for myself, others, and the situation," she explained. Julie had a mindfulness practice going into this situation, and her practice of these skills in everyday moments allowed her to bring them into more critical experiences such as this one.

If you don't yet have evidence that your body has your back, it may be difficult even to begin the journey toward greater embodiment. Pillar 5, which covers trust and integration, will help. For now, start small. Use the exercises at the end of this pillar to assist you.

When you start to gather evidence that courage works, it's easier to continue to take risks and practice courage more regularly. Each time you courageously choose to consult your body and follow its wisdom, you gain evidence that it's okay to leap in big or small ways. You teach yourself that things work out, even if it doesn't necessarily feel that way in the moment.

Melissa's courage has allowed her to continually play bigger and have a greater impact, by giving her body the experience of being safe, even through discomfort, over and over again. She keeps widening her window of resilience and giving herself opportunities to remember that her body has her back. Because of this, more people get to experience her message and be changed through her story.

Consider how you present yourself in your life.

- Where are you holding back from courageously showing up more fully?

- Is there a part of you that you keep under the radar, say at work or with friends?

- Can you bring a recent situation to mind where you have experienced some dissonance between your inner and outer worlds?

When you grow the courage to trust the amazing integrated mind-body organism that is *you*, everything gets easier.

Exercises to Bring Your Body on Board

Reflect on risk

How much risk are you willing to accept in order to live the life you want to live? How do you know if your body agrees with your perceived comfort level for risk? We face risks in all areas of our lives—personal, interpersonal, professional, financial. Let's start with something very concrete: money.

Think about your current level of financial security and what risks you may need to take to achieve your goals. For example, you might decide you need to quit your job to start your own business. What are the risks, and what does it feel like in your body when you think about these risks? Consider ways you can mitigate the most important risks, and notice if anything changes in your body.

Now for something a bit more personal: your relationships. Think about a relationship you are trying to grow and what might be at stake. For example, you may run the risk of being rejected. What does it feel like in your body when you think about these risks? Consider ways you can mitigate the most important risks and notice if anything changes in your body.

Reflect on this experience in your journal, or share it with a friend or partner.

Explore what courage feels like in your body

Allow yourself to enter into a safe space where you feel comfortable to spend five or ten minutes. This could be a private space in your home—even the bathroom if that is what's available. It might be your office, or outside in nature.

Take three slow, gentle breaths, in through your nose and out through your mouth or nose. If you feel comfortable doing so, close your eyes, or you may prefer to soften your gaze but keep your eyes open.

Ask yourself: "What does courage feel like in my body? When I am called to be brave, what happens in my body?" Pause and witness. What are you feeling? Where are you noticing something coming up in your body? How might you describe the quality or characteristics of these sensations— big or small, dark or bright, moving or still, heavy or light?

Pause and give your body a shake. Take three more slow, gentle breaths.

Repeat the exercise a few times, especially if the signals are not clear. To get a clearer signal, you may want to bring to mind a memory of when you had to be brave despite your fear. Maybe you had to stand up to your boss when they were being unfair to your colleague, or you called out someone who was being a bully. Come back to how that felt in your body.

Reflect on this experience in your journal, or share it with a trusted other.

Tap into your intuition

Your intuition is one of the ways your body communicates with you. This information does not come to you in the form of rational thoughts. Instead, you receive images, sensations, and feelings that are generated by neurons outside the brain, in the body, often in the heart and gut. This bodily information often comes in response to what is going on in your mind or in your environment. We all have access to our intuition, but many of us have not been paying attention to it. The following is a simple exercise to tap into your body instincts.

Begin by thinking about a difficult conversation you want or need to have. Play it out in your mind. Allow yourself to think about different scenarios of how the talk could go.

Now, ask yourself, "What is the best way for me to have this conversation?"

Take a deep inhale, and exhale, and go through the scenarios in your mind again. Start to observe what is coming up in your body as you move from one scenario to the next. Pay particular attention to sensations in your heart and your gut.

Ask yourself the question again: "What is the best way for me to have this conversation?" Allow the answer to start to take shape in your mind.

If you find it difficult to get any signals from your body while doing this exercise, try it with a simpler question, such as "What do I want for dinner?" By regularly tapping into your body's signals, you will slowly build up your capacity to access your intuition.

PILLAR 4

Consciously Connecting with Yourself and Others

In a world of increasingly complex problems, **embodiment allows you to bridge the gap between simply working together and truly collaborating.**

JESSE EXPRESSED THEIR experience of embodying the Explorer style when they shared, "I didn't realize how much healing I have left to do around my body, even though my transition took place years ago." Jesse is a passionate transgender community leader who is studying to become a psychologist. When asked about their perspective on embodiment, they answered: "It's complex for me. I have all these suppressed memories of my life pre-transition, but in learning how to bring awareness to my body, I've connected deeper with myself, and those memories have been returning to me." They continued, demonstrating qualities of the Connector: "I know it is important to do this healing work around my body for me to feel whole, but it's also important for my community. When people transition, it takes time to realize how much their physical changes impact their mental, emotional, and spiritual well-being. Other people in my community have had similar experiences to me and when I can connect with myself and my body in these raw and brave ways, I'm better at empathizing and supporting others. I really believe this work helps us be kinder to one another. We lead as a community, rather than one person at the top having all the power."

True leadership is a process, expressed through action, and is not meant to be done in isolation. "We need to use our voices as an act of leadership," Jesse said, embodying the Integrator, "and know when to step back and let others use their voices too. To do that, we need to be connected to and grounded in our bodies. It's an ongoing process."

As you engage with your life and your leadership, you may notice a need to connect with yourself and others in more conscious, collaborative, and communal ways. Neuro-scientist Matthew Lieberman points out that connection is one of our most basic needs, and that our brains react to the pain of disconnection in the same way we react to physical pain. Our brains are wired to be social, to be in connection with others, and to live and lead alongside others. You may, however, feel that you have to do it on your own, as though you have to demonstrate that you are strong enough, good enough, and worthy of your success. Perhaps you feel you have to suffer your mistakes and failures alone? Stanford University's Bill Burnett and Dave Evans, in their book *Designing Your Life*, challenge us to reframe our thinking—to see ourselves, our careers, and our lives as communal efforts, as something that we build together.

In this pillar, we guide you to explore your inner environment as well as the outer environments that support you in connecting. You will also learn about relationship attachment styles, which attachment style you embody, and how this affects connection. You will then tap into your body's sensations to set healthy boundaries, so that you can lead in a connected and collaborative way, rather than a disconnected, lonely, and competitive way. We end by exploring how embodiment helps us to work together more meaningfully, and how leading embodied teams is an increasingly important competency in addressing current and future challenges.

Mastering Your Internal and External Environments

Conscious connection with yourself and others requires mastery over your internal and external environments. To master your internal environment means to expand your capacity to self-regulate. The first three pillars of this book speak to various self-regulation tools and practices. This pillar looks at regulation in relation to others, or co-regulation.

You are built to be a social being. You are not supposed to do humanness alone. It is natural to depend on the external world and on others to co-regulate. Co-regulation means to attune to another being or group of beings in order to experience a positive shift in your nervous system. In fact, co-regulation is the basis for self-regulation. You need healthy relationships with your external environment, the things that you consume, and the people around you in order to function and lead optimally.

Your external environment

Have you ever noticed that you feel more relaxed, have greater clarity of mind, and are more able to connect with yourself and others in some environments as opposed to others? Or that certain environments are more appropriate for certain contexts? The quality of water, food, air, light, and sound in your environment affects your well-being, and your capacity to be embodied. In the same way, there are unique environmental factors that contribute to, or detract from, your capacity to connect with yourself and others.

Casey worked in a coworking space for four years. After running her online business from home, going somewhere for work was a pleasure. "When I walked through the elevator doors, the open space, big windows, unlimited coffee, and sight of busy entrepreneurs would put me in my creative zone," she said. It was the perfect environment for her to feel embodied and inspired to do her work … at the beginning.

But as time went on, Casey's business changed, and so did the space.

She found herself facilitating deeper conversations with her clients, helping them process difficult emotions as they navigated big changes in their lives, which required a quieter environment as she guided them into their bodies. She started to feel that this was challenging to do in a rented boardroom, with hustle and bustle right outside the door.

Though Casey was happy for the owner and for the community that more members were joining the coworking space, it was becoming too busy for her. "If I didn't arrive early enough, other members would occupy my go-to desk, and the only quiet spaces were constantly booked. My mind-body and nervous system couldn't settle, since the consistency I once had was gone. For a week straight, pain started to shoot through my back every time I sat down to work." The physical dysregulation led to emotional dysregulation, and she simply could no longer relax or "get in the zone" at work.

That's when she knew it was time to move on. "When I packed up my stuff and walked out of the space, I felt relieved. And the pain in my back dissipated, almost immediately," Casey recalled.

Take a moment to consider your key external environments: home, office, commute to work, coworking space, boardroom, outdoor space, and so on.

- What is something that helps you connect with yourself and others in your environment?

- What do you feel in your body when you are in an environment that nourishes you?

- What is one thing in your environment that depletes you?

- How does your environment need to change as your context or situation changes?

There are very likely smells, sounds, sights, or objects that influence how you feel. For Julie, higher-pitched sounds are agitating to her nervous system. An example: she can tell herself rationally that it's just a dog whining, but such sounds still send her down her autonomic ladder.

What you consume

What you consume makes a difference too. The food you eat, the media you take in, the substances you ingest—all have an influence on your capacity to consciously connect with yourself and others. They can nourish or deplete your inner resources. Consuming food that offers you sustained energy can make a big difference in how you react to the people around you. Can you relate to being indecisive and short with others when you are "hangry"?

What you take in through the news or social media can empower and inspire you, or it can send you down your autonomic ladder. Of course, drugs and alcohol also affect how you connect. Perhaps you've used a glass of wine or whiskey as a social lubricant, only to observe after a few refills that it has the opposite effect.

What nourishes you under one circumstance could deplete you in another. For example, watching Netflix could offer you an opportunity to slow down and relax your mind-body in a way that leaves you feeling refreshed, connected with yourself, and filled up. In another moment, it could easily turn into a mindless binge that leaves you feeling worse, less connected to yourself, more depleted than before, and isolated from others.

On the whole, what do you consume that supports you? What do you consume that does not support you?

The people around you

Have you ever worked on a team with a person who somehow seemed to suck the life out of a room? We invite you to bring that person to mind, just for a moment. How do you feel even thinking about them? This is the type of person you catch complaining, rebutting new ideas, and responding to work and life from a "glass half empty" point of view. Being with them feels draining and constrictive, and can facilitate more tension or discomfort building in your body.

Now think about someone who is a delight to work with—your absolute favorite leader, or the person who has had the most positive impact on your life. How do you feel just thinking about them? How do you feel when they walk into a room? How would you describe the energy they embody? Does this person's presence create expansion in you? Do you walk away from meetings with them feeling calm, confident, and able to create? Their leadership likely inspires and motivates, and not just because of what they do, but also because of who they are and the energy they embody.

You may have heard the expression "you are the average of the five people you spend the most time with," attributed to motivational speaker Jim Rohn. We agree with organizational psychologist David Burkus that, rather, you are the average of ALL the people who surround you. Have you noticed that who you spend time with doesn't just influence your thinking and behavior but also affects how you feel inside your own body?

Embodied Leaders know that they influence their own bodies and the bodies of others. They know—in some cases intuitively—that to be the best versions of themselves and connect consciously with others, they need to feel authentic, attuned, safe, and secure in their bodies. They also know that through their presence they can help other people feel safe too.

Jesse shared that since they began their deeper healing through embodiment, they have felt more safe and secure in their body and nervous system, even around folks who don't quite understand their lived experience. They still feel triggered in moments, but have more connecting conversations, even about sensitive topics such as transphobia and discrimination, with more consciousness and less reactivity. Jesse can see how these deeper, more challenging conversations bring different types of people together and create more allies and support for their community. Jesse has also realized that to lean into leading those hard conversations, they need to be supported by friends and colleagues whom they feel safe with and encouraged by—the ones who help to keep their cup full.

You can intentionally co-regulate with others who may be in different states to help them feel safe and social too.

The top of the autonomic ladder is often referred to as the safe and social state, for good reason. When people feel safe, they can better engage with others consciously. As an Embodied Leader, when you are consciously aware of being in your safe and social state, you can intentionally co-regulate with others who may be in different states to help them feel safe and social, too, so that connection and leadership can take place in a meaningful way. You are metaphorically extending your hand to pull them up the ladder.

In practical terms, this could look like consciously deepening your breath, maintaining eye contact, speaking with a more relaxed tone, and even offering a teammate touch (if appropriate) through a handshake or arm squeeze to soothe your teammate's stressed and agitated nervous system.

When faced with a difficult conversation, Courtney shared, "I will take slower, deeper breaths in the presence of the person I am speaking with and physically connect to the ground or to an object so that I stay with my senses, until I feel my heartbeat slow down, and I feel myself shifting from fight-or-flight to safe and social." If Courtney feels herself going back to fight-or-flight or if she senses this shift in the other person, she will repeat the sequence. If that seems to trigger in them even greater agitation, she might straighten her spine and breathe deeply but a bit faster, to match their energy and guide them back. Courtney reflected: "If I anticipate that this might be an issue, I may suggest a walking meeting instead, so that we can use movement to co-regulate."

Courtney has also chosen to pause a conversation if she or the other person cannot find their way to a connected state. Very little of what we say when in fight-or-flight, freeze, or shutdown will stick anyway. There is also the risk that biases triggered by fear will lessen our ability to correctly interpret what is being shared, leading to potential damage to the relationship.

As an Embodied Leader, when you feel yourself agitated or shutdown, you can bring your awareness to either of those dysregulated states and then seek what you need to regulate, either on your own or with the support of others. For example, you could take a walk in nature, practice a helpful breathing technique, or call a good friend to talk it out.

And remember, you don't have to be in another person's physical presence to experience the positive impact on your nervous system. You can even think about a person you love, listen to a podcast with someone whose voice is soothing, or co-regulate with another through a screen.

Consider your life right now.

- With whom do you feel at ease? Is it with a family member? A close friend? Your pet? A colleague?

- Who do you spend the most time with? Who would you like to spend more time with?

- And who would it be helpful to spend less time with or to spend time with in a different way?

Context matters

What is too much of any one thing? How much is enough? The right amount depends on your context. Being embodied facilitates you checking in with yourself in any given moment for what you might need. Your body is like an instrument, regularly needing to be retuned depending on various internal and external conditions.

Let's go back to your window of resilience. Each stressor you encounter in a day, be it from a hectic environment, the media you consume, or the person who drains your energy, has the potential to shrink your window. While you don't want to—and can't—control all the variables, when you look for ways to optimize your internal and external environments, you help your window widen, and create more capacity for connection and for thriving amidst stress and adversity. The goal is not to widen your window to take on more and more stress, but rather to allow more space for situations that are outside your control. When your window is wide, unexpected circumstances can show up without overwhelming your capacity to remain safe, secure, and connected.

Even small changes in your internal and external environments can shift how you function in a meaningful way, and help you create a more productive, conscious connection with yourself and with the people you lead.

Your Body Feels Your Relationship Attachment Style

As you are discovering, how you connect with others is influenced by a host of factors—and an important one that you may not be aware of is your relationship attachment style. Attachment theory is a psychological framework that speaks to the relationships and bonds between people. The prominent psychologist John Bowlby defined attachment as a "lasting psychological connectedness between human beings."

There are four main attachment styles that can be viewed across different relationships, from childhood with primary caregivers to friendships, romantic relationships, and relationships within a work context. Attachment theory itself suggests that being aware of attachment styles can help regulate your nervous system, improve your ability to communicate, and leverage your inner state to take action and be a better leader.

Understanding attachment theory, particularly through the lens of embodiment, will support the way you connect with yourself and others, and improve your ability to lead.

Consider these four options and reflect honestly. What would you say is your general pattern in relationships right now?

- I find it easy to get close to others. I am comfortable relying on others, and I am not highly anxious about being abandoned or developing intimacy.

- I am not comfortable getting close to others or relying on them, and I place significant importance on independence and self-sufficiency.

- I want to be close, but often closer than others would like, and I experience significant anxiety about being abandoned.

- I want to be close to others and yet avoid closeness for fear of getting hurt. I experience high anxiety and avoidance.

If you see yourself in the first option, your primary attachment style may be *secure*. If you identify more with the second, your primary attachment style may be *avoidant*. The third option is indicative of an *anxious* attachment style, while the fourth is suggestive of a *fearful avoidant* attachment style. You may feel secure in one relationship while anxious or avoidant in another. In fact, this is very likely.

Notice what happens in your body as you connect with one of these options. Please know that if you resonate with an insecure attachment style (options two, three, or four), your attachment style is not something you chose; instead, it developed as a result of growing up in an environment that did not provide the consistent support you needed. Unfortunately, this experience is common. Becoming more embodied asks that you take responsibility for your attachment patterns in relationships and that you become aware of how attachment plays out in relationships and in your leadership. Through this process, you will develop more secure and healthy ways of relating.

Let's take a closer look at these various attachment styles, focusing on how they feel in your body when activated. For each style, an example is provided of what this might look like for a leader being called in by a superior for a rather significant mistake made under their responsibility. These examples assume a context in which a superior is acting in a respectful and reasonable manner. Harassment, a far too common situation in workplaces, would be triggering for anyone, irrespective of their attachment style. Leadership styles that are associated with micromanaging and other harmful approaches are also likely to activate insecure attachment patterns in relationships.

Attachment and Your Body

Secure attachment and your body

Secure attachment looks like being comfortable depending on others as well as being alone. Feeling secure means to be in your safe and social state, which is typically described as feeling relaxed, calm, and grounded in your body, while remaining focused, alert, and awake. Your mind-body and nervous system are optimally aroused and you feel relatively safe in your relationships, even when situations become emotional or vulnerable.

A leader with a secure attachment style is more likely to stay grounded and calm even when they sense strong emotions surging through their body while being called in to account for a mistake.

Avoidant attachment and your body

Avoidant attachment mimics hypo-arousal, or a shutdown response in your body. When things get stressful in relationships, you may tend to avoid potentially uncomfortable conversations, to disengage, and to resort to self-regulation rather than co-regulation. A person with an avoidant style tends to be overly self-reliant and to suppress emotions rather than feel the feelings move through their body.

When called in to account for a mistake, a leader with an avoidant attachment style may shut down at the criticism, may shut out the other person by crossing their arms, and may notice after the encounter that they can't recall the details of what was said.

Anxious attachment and your body

Anxious attachment mimics hyper-arousal or the fight-or-flight response in your body. Your sympathetic nervous system is activated when you feel anxiously attached. This could result in an elevated heart rate, butterflies in your stomach, or even an increase in your body temperature. There may be triggers from outside that activate a feeling of insecurity and/or stories in your mind that leave you feeling insecure. When this style is activated, you will likely feel less emotionally regulated. This may show up in the body as an uncomfortable inner experience—lots of energy moving internally, tears, or even shaking or hyperventilating.

A leader with an anxious attachment style may feel defensive at the criticism, may want to physically move away from the encounter, and may feel shame or place blame solely on themselves for the mistake. They may also be overly concerned about what the other person thinks of them, and what impact this mistake may have on the impression that others hold of them.

Fearful-avoidant attachment and your body

People with the fearful-avoidant attachment style experience a combination of anxious attachment and avoidant attachment. In certain relationships, they oscillate between wanting closeness and feeling anxious sensations in their body about getting close, and feeling shutdown or numb in their body as they detach and return to a state of hyper-independence.

A leader with a fearful-avoidant attachment style who receives criticism may go into defensive mode while at the same time looking for validation from their superior. If the validation is not forthcoming, the leader may start to shut down and seek to detach from the encounter.

What facilitates secure relating?

It was once believed that your attachment style was fixed. If you were insecure in your attachment style as a child, you were destined to be insecure in all relationships as an adult. Current research, however, suggests that your attachment style can change, and that you can develop new relational patterns within healthy relationships.

Developing awareness by attuning to your body, engaging in a self-reflection practice, and getting support through therapy or coaching can help you move to a more secure attachment style. Knowing your attachment style, and noticing that it varies across relationships, allows you to see more clearly when you are triggered, and to mindfully observe how your nervous system reacts and the sensations that come up in your body. This awareness can then help you choose more consciously what to do next.

It is also very helpful for people with insecure attachment styles to spend time with people who exhibit more secure attachment styles, as they can co-regulate and model more healthy and productive coping behaviors. Remember, you become the people you spend the most time with, so choose wisely!

Yes, You Might Need Better Boundaries

Boundaries reflect the limits—physical and psychological—that you set for yourself and your relationships. They are grounded in your values and beliefs, as well as your lived experiences. Boundaries are dependent on cultural and other contextual factors. They are not static, and they can change and evolve depending on context and circumstance. They can also vary from relationship to relationship, depending on established trust and understanding.

For instance, Julie has people with whom she can share anything and has a deep sense of trust that she will not be judged, that information will not be used against her, and that she will be met with support. She noted, "There are also people in my life who are supportive and significant, but with whom I filter more of what I share, holding my cards more closely." Noticing and tuning into her body's wisdom has allowed her to navigate boundaries in different relationships in order to respect this critical need for safety.

Signs that you have healthy boundaries may include:

- You stand up for what is important to you.

- You accept when others set a limit, such as saying no.

- You disclose personal information appropriately, rather than over- or under-sharing.

- You respect an important self-boundary even when you feel guilty about doing so.

- You set consequences for others when your limits are not respected.

Saying no to something you would be good at but do not have interest in, or time for, can be a really tough boundary to set. You may feel pride for having been asked, worry about disappointing the other person, and fear that if you say no, you will not be asked again. Setting a clear boundary requires that you know when you will benefit from acting on a request, and when saying no is the best answer for you. As author and public speaker Greg McKeown writes in his book *Essentialism,* "The difference between successful people and very successful people is that very successful people say 'no' to almost everything."

Signs that your boundaries need to be reinforced may include:

- You do not clearly communicate your needs.

- You feel resentful when your needs are not being met.

- You find it difficult to make your own choices or know what you want.

- You easily take on other people's feelings or challenges.

- You worry and feel anxious about disappointing others and about belonging.

Having porous or unclear boundaries can make it difficult to connect with yourself and with others because you are not clearly communicating the rules of engagement. When you and those around you know the rules, everyone feels more safe and secure, and it is more likely that everyone will stay in a safe and social state. Healthy boundaries involve giving in relationships without self-sacrificing. They involve not losing yourself.

Boundaries and leadership

As a leader, you play an important role in modeling healthy boundaries and boundary setting, and in clarifying expectations around boundaries for your team or context.

Boundary setting in leadership is critical not only to your own well-being but also to the psychological safety and security of those around you. Whether you lead a company, a team, a community group, or a family, people look to you for a sense of what is important, what is expected, what is okay, and what is not okay. Clear and consistent boundaries make us all feel safe, whereas lack of clarity, inconsistency, and contradictions can lead to anxiety, fear, or even apathy.

When you and those around you know the rules, **everyone feels more safe and secure.**

How many times have you been in a situation where a leader says they are committed to a certain behavior but acts in a different way? What has that felt like in your body?

Boundaries and the body

Because boundaries help you feel safe, secure, connected, and aligned with your values, when your body is on board, it will send you clear signals if you or someone else breaches your boundaries. These signals can also be useful in helping clarify and establish your boundaries, as your body will tell you what matters most. Getting in touch with what "no" feels like in your body can be an excellent first step in either establishing or reinforcing your healthy boundaries.

Whatever boundaries you choose, know that this space is not black or white. Healthy boundaries are firm and flexible, somewhere between porous and rigid. Boundaries are within your control, and practicing healthy boundary setting will revolutionize your relationships with yourself and with others.

What does "no" feel like in your body?

It is okay if you don't know what saying no feels like in your body just yet. Saying no is hard.

Casey shared: "I often feel a 'no' present as tightness around my heart space or a constriction in my throat. Sometimes, when I feel extra vulnerable, my heart rate starts to increase, my breathing becomes shorter and sharper, and my face starts to turn red." This is her body's autonomic nervous system reacting to her long-standing history of sacrificing herself to please others. Saying no is hard for a recovering "people pleaser," but when she practices listening to her body and acting upon its wisdom, it gets easier.

This tightness in her chest, constriction in her throat, and/or elevated heart rate tell her that she needs to set a boundary. If she doesn't, the sensations typically become more prominent and ultimately lead to her feeling drained of energy, bitter, or even resentful. It has taken awhile, but she has learned that the false sense of belonging that she gets from people-pleasing is not worth it. Catching this and setting different boundaries allow her to get back to home base, an embodied and present state. Boundaries are often hard to set in the moment because they feel uncomfortable in the short term. But in the long term, they often feel expansive and freeing.

If saying no is easy for you or you've had lots of practice, you may be able to do so in a very calm, grounded, and mindful way. If saying no is difficult for you, rest assured that this is a skill that you can and will learn with practice. We have included an exercise on this at the end of this pillar. Remember, whatever you practice will grow stronger!

Setting boundaries, by saying no or in other ways, allows you to respond with integrity and frees up energy so you can do the things you really want to do. Creating this space will help you feel open and centered, so that you can connect and lead more consciously. Boundaries will also help you focus on your purpose and contribution, which we will discuss in Pillar 6.

Collaboration and Co-creation

The challenges that leaders face in today's world are increasingly complex. When global consulting firm Grant Thornton asked senior managers what attributes leaders would require for the future, they highlighted adaptation, ability to innovate, empathy, and collaboration. Leaders today are being called to collaborate in new ways, and to foster collaborative environments designed to help people feel safe, secure, and valued in the collaboration, so they can bring their best selves forward.

As Jesse emphasized, we need each other in order to accomplish great things. We need new ways to organize ourselves, and we need to work together to build the trust, engagement, and safety required so that individuals will risk offering their best ideas and most authentic contributions. We need to create spaces for deep, messy conversations, and build resilience to sit with the discomfort and vulnerability that come from being curious and open, and from bringing diverse perspectives to the table.

Embodied Leaders create the conditions for this type of collaboration to emerge and sustain itself. In *Resonate: Zen and the Way of Making a Difference*, Ginny Whitelaw, Zen Roshi and founder of the Institute for Zen Leadership, describes the need for leaders to attune to the conditions (including people) around them, find a rhythm that matches those conditions, and drive that rhythm by using the right energy pattern at the right time. When groups work together in this way—and when they face intense, unifying challenges together with appropriate supports—they can enter into coherence or team flow, which allows the efforts of individuals to be amplified, the sense of individualism to be temporarily reduced, and their collaboration and co-creation to shift to a new level. Being embodied allows individuals and groups to enter into coherence more easily and to bring each other into higher levels of collaboration and co-creation.

In a world of increasingly complex problems, embodiment allows us to bridge the gap between simply working together and truly collaborating.

Exercises to Bring Your Body on Board

Use inside and outside tools

Andrew Huberman, a neuroscientist and professor at Stanford University, has provided a useful distinction between inside and outside tools; in other words, tools that come from within and tools from external sources. Some examples of inside tools are breathwork, imagination, and visualization. Examples of outside tools include your environment—such as optimizing lighting in your home or adding plants—your diet, or taking a weekly walk with a friend.

Consider one inside or outside tool that might be the most useful right now in helping you grow your connection with yourself and/or others.

Set an intention to implement this tool for the next week, such as doing a five- to ten-minute breathwork practice each morning or dimming the lights each evening.

What does "no" feel like in your body?

Bring to mind a situation when you said yes but wish you had said no. Perhaps you said yes out of a sense of obligation, or just by default. Don't worry about whether it was the "right" or "wrong" thing to do. Just bring the situation to mind and honor it.

Close your eyes, and put yourself back in that situation. Remember all that you can about it. Drop into your body.

Focus on the moment right before you said yes. What do you feel right now in your body and where do you feel it? Does your body feel expansive or restrictive? Does your body feel calm or nervous? Does your body feel enthusiastic or drained?

Now, replay the exact scenario in your mind's eye one more time. Just like before, close your eyes and drop into your body. Come back to the moment right before you said yes, but now imagine saying no. What does that feel like in your body? What sensations do you notice, and where do you feel them?

Use these insights to identify opportunities that would further support your well-being. This may mean identifying and setting different boundaries with certain individuals.

Practice saying no or yes based on what you feel.

Deepen your collaboration through co-creation

Co-creating requires us to let go of control, self-consciousness, and ego. By giving in to the creative process, you can experience team flow, and deepen your collaborative relationships and results. This practice focuses on co-writing, but you could adapt it to other collaborative endeavors.

Choose a co-writing partner.

Decide on a topic you will write about. It should be something that you both have knowledge about or expertise in and that will require you to push the boundaries of that knowledge further.

Decide on the goal, process, and time you will spend doing this. For instance, the goal could be producing a short article to publish on social media. The process might be defining a short outline together and deciding who will take the first crack at what elements of the outline. You might agree on a time of twenty to thirty minutes of writing before switching sections.

Commit to two or three co-writing sessions, or continue until your product is complete.

Note: co-writing sessions should allow for concentration on the task at hand. Consider what you need. For instance, you may want to go for a walk beforehand, start the session with a short meditation, or play music to help focus.

Reflect together on the process. What issues came up, and how did they feel in your body? What benefits emerged? What did you each learn?

Celebrate the completion of your co-written product! Consider letting your readers know about your co-creation process and what you both learned from this experience.

Trusting and Integrating Body Wisdom

If you ignore parts of yourself you can't accept, **your mind-body will sense this and keep you in fear, control, and distrust.**

DALILA IS A diversity, equity, and inclusion coach and consultant for entrepreneurs and organizations. She helps them to clarify their values as they relate to advocacy and inclusion and then to do the deep work of aligning their businesses with those values. When asked about the transformations she has experienced in leadership, and how embodiment has played a role, she got personal: "I was raised by a woman that had a large amount of trauma, including big trust issues. She inadvertently passed them on to me. She told me, 'Women don't want to be your friend. They don't want to support you.' And I believed her—I took on this untruth as truth."

Dalila shared that she would feel all kinds of discomfort in her body when attempting to work with women in a collaborative way. Her heart rate would increase, she'd start to feel hot, and she'd experience an overall sensation of uneasiness. She embodied the characteristics of the Explorer, as she would disconnect and protect herself in these experiences, and for understandable reasons. She disclosed: "I felt so uncomfortable when I tried to collaborate with other women that I would end the connection or find some way to go back to working alone. But I started to notice how isolated I would end up feeling when I cut myself off from these collaborative experiences. I would watch how other women could create joint efforts together to grow their businesses or serve people in bigger and more powerful ways, and it made me want to dig into why it was so hard for me."

She began to challenge herself to stay present even when she felt the discomfort in her body, and worked through, with a therapist, this pattern of not trusting. In other words, she began to embody the Connector.

She continued: "I needed to heal from this intergenerational belief system so that I could find more connection in my life and business. I also wanted to heal to better support my clients on their journeys. I had to find examples of trust among women, and notice how I felt in my body when it was present. I had to stop being limited by my mother's trauma. Now I can better collaborate, rather than compete, and feel more integrated in my work." Dalila now embodies the Integrator more often. She leads with openness, vulnerability, and trust in her interactions, and is more masterful at creating experiences of trust, even when navigating instances of racism or inequity in the workplace.

Our early experiences are so important in shaping who we become as adults, and as leaders. We (Courtney, Julie, and Casey) have a common experience of being introduced to leadership roles early in our lives. We cared for younger siblings or other family members and were asked to take on responsibilities at home, on the farm, or at school. We played key roles on family projects or within the family business. Early experiences of responsibility and trust contributed to forming each of us, and helped us see how we fed into a greater, integrated whole. At the same time, since these experiences happened in our formative years, later disentangling which responsibilities belonged to us and which belonged to others was difficult, as was recognizing that our identities were about more than just being the ones who could be trusted to get things done.

Integration from a leadership perspective is about letting all of you show up, authentically and vulnerably, and creating space for others to show up as well. This opens up the possibility of trust—trusting yourself and others, and trusting that you have value and worth beyond your responsibilities and competencies. In the words of the legendary psychiatrist Carl Jung, "wholeness is not achieved by cutting off a portion of one's being, but by integration of the contraries." When you create spaces where others feel comfortable being their full, integrated selves, innovation, productivity, and fulfillment soon follow. We naturally seek out leaders who create these spaces because of a desire to be in a trusting environment where we can be ourselves and develop our full potential. Authentic, trusted leaders play key roles in the lives of their friends, families, and neighbors, not just in the workplace.

This pillar is about trust and integration. Trust is not just a cognitive frame but a felt sense in your body, influenced by the biases of your lived experience. Trust, in your own body wisdom and in other people, is a prerequisite for becoming a more integrated version of yourself, while also creating integrated and cohesive teams, work cultures, and collective growth. We will explore the conditions that open up the possibility of trust, and how to notice, open, and shift toward greater cohesion and integration.

What Is Trust?

Trust is a necessary feature of our collective, connected life as humans.

You trust because it makes rational sense to do so—it is at the foundation of your capacity to work with others and achieve more than you could otherwise. You also trust because your psychological and physical well-being is tied to your ability to find safety and security through intra- and interpersonal relationships. Stephen Porges describes our two fundamental human needs as those of safety and of connection. Trust is essential to survival.

Trust can also be thought of as a bit of a *shortcut*, a way for your nervous system to cope with complexity and help you make decisions more quickly and easily, while keeping you safe and secure in the process. You form a template in your mind around trust (or distrust) to create structure and stability in your interpretation of a situation or relationship. This template is called a cognitive frame. Once formed, this frame is pretty stable and functions as a decisional shortcut. The frame only changes if significant new experiences give you reason to readjust, toward either more trust or less trust.

You already have a cognitive frame around trust that filters your perceptions of others' intentions, motivations, behaviors, and trustworthiness. You also have a somatic frame around trust, which we will discuss further below. The people you lead also have their own frames, different from each other, and grounded in their individual experiences. The exercises around trust included at the end of this pillar aim to shift your cognitive and somatic frames toward greater levels of trust. As you become more and more embodied, you will see that trusting yourself and others is a dynamic, evolving process that requires vulnerability, intentionality, and experience. Trust is earned and can be lost. Through trial and error, you learn how to use your body's wisdom to fairly assess trustworthiness, and to hold space for building trust.

In her book *Dare to Lead*, Brené Brown talks about the ingredients necessary for trust. One of those is being willing to "extend the most generous interpretation possible to the intentions, words, and actions of others." Although we agree with this ingredient, we wonder whether being able to do this is at least in part a function of privilege, and whether those who have been marginalized, oppressed, and abused might find it difficult, if not impossible, to start from this place of vulnerability.

As a leader, you are responsible for creating safe and trusting spaces for others, especially those who have less power than you do, whether by virtue of their position in the organization or because of another aspect of their identity. As you learned in Pillars 2 and 4, part of the way leaders do this is by having a regulated nervous system to which others can co-regulate. As author, master coach, and trauma specialist Resmaa Menakem highlights in his book *My Grandmother's Hands*, "A settled body enables you to harmonize and connect with other bodies around you, while encouraging those bodies to settle as well... A calm, settled body is the foundation for health, for healing, for helping others, and for changing the world." It is important to acknowledge that it is a privilege to have the knowledge and skills required to self-regulate, and that those who have experienced trauma, disempowerment, or marginalization may have a more difficult journey toward trust.

Trust as something that happens in the body

Trust is not just a cognitive frame—something in the mind— but also a somatic frame, a felt experience in the body. Trust (or distrust) is something that happens in the body, often outside your conscious awareness. It is a signal from your mind-body that a situation or person is safe, or that you should proceed with caution. Before she chose to heal, Dalila's somatic frame told her it wasn't safe to deeply connect or collaborate with other women.

Your body picks up on trust signals through actions, words, body language, and context. These signals are interpreted through your somatic frame, and you add this information to that of your previous experiences. Your mind-body interprets these data and "tells" you, through felt sense in the body, whether or not it is safe to trust.

When experienced in the body, trust might feel like instantly being comfortable with a new colleague ("I feel like I've known them for years!") or feeling relaxed in a new environment ("I'm getting a good vibe from this place"). You have likely experienced someone having this type of calming effect on you, where their presence, energy, voice, or some other quality puts you at ease. Distrust, in contrast, might feel like having your pulse or your breath pick up speed when you meet someone new ("something about her made me feel intimidated"). Stephen Porges refers to this felt sense in the body as neuroception. It is like a "spidey sense" for when, what, and whom you can trust.

While this feedback system is very useful, it is important to remember that your cognitive frame and your somatic frame are prone to bias. This is true for all of us. For instance, you may have lived through traumatic experiences that eroded trust for you. Even if a person or situation is safe, your mind-body may be sending you mixed signals that are more difficult to interpret. Importantly, this is true for those around you as well, and you can learn how to foster trust by noticing how their bodies react to your words, actions, and body language as you engage with them.

As a concrete example, Courtney recalls an exercise during her most recent yoga teacher training where the instructor asked everyone to stand at opposite ends of a room, facing a partner. Partner A would signal to partner B across from them to step forward with a wave, and to stop by placing both hands down. Partner A was guided to listen to their body to know when to ask partner B to advance or to stop.

Courtney described her experience: "I had connected with my partner during the training, and I felt she was trustworthy. But as she advanced, I felt my whole body constrict. I had to use my breath to release the constriction before asking her to come closer." Up until the end of the exercise, Courtney felt discomfort in her body. When she and her partner reflected on the exercise, her partner shared that she was getting strong signals from Courtney to not move forward, which she did not understand. She knew that Courtney trusted her and that they had a good relationship.

So what was going on? "In discussing this exercise with my psychologist," Courtney shared, "we concluded that my body was sending signals *not* based on my direct experience of this person, but rather based on wiring that caused me to be cautious of creating connections with other people, for fear of being rejected or abandoned." This insight into the signals that Courtney's body sends around connection has made her much more self-aware and mindful of how she is with others, and has helped her to overcome barriers to connection that she didn't even realize were there before.

Similarly, Dalila's desire to overcome her trust issues with other women led her to set an intention. She would go to networking events for business leaders and lean into her vulnerability and discomfort when it showed up. For a while, she practiced just noticing her body and giving it an experience of feeling safe when meeting new people. She gave herself permission to take her time with developing those new connections, so that trust could build slowly. She began to collaborate on projects with women she met. She started on small ones rather than jumping into big ones, and gave herself the experience of feeling good. After a while, she came to love the support she felt and the synergy that was built through collaboration. She started a podcast with another woman, invited women as guest speakers for her clients, and was invited into new opportunities to share her work with others.

What about you? Can you recall a time or situation when your body has signaled caution, and upon later reflection you realized that it was a response to something in your past, rather than an unsafe situation in the present moment? Remember, we do not choose our biologically driven responses. Our autonomic nervous system chooses for us.

Self-trust as something worth developing

Many leaders struggle with self-doubt, insecurities, and not feeling as though they are worthy or enough. While a healthy dose of self-doubt can be grounding and help you avoid the blinders of overconfidence, chronic self-doubt can erode your confidence and trust in yourself. When you lose trust in yourself, you lose the belief that you can rely on yourself and keep yourself safe and secure. You stay in the mode of seeking knowledge, skills, and solutions to feel safe and secure. When you don't feel safe and secure, your body reacts, and so do the bodies of those around you.

As we discussed in Pillar 4, the environments that you expose yourself to can also contribute to this erosion. For instance, we now understand that "impostor syndrome"—self-doubt that cannot be justified by evidence—is not just about what you think of yourself but also about environmental factors and biases that elicit these feelings.

What can show up on the surface as overconfidence is often a reaction to self-doubt. Depending on your attachment pattern in a particular context or relationship, the way you present yourself will look different, and yet all humans share an underlying fear of vulnerability and need for connection.

Trust in yourself is important to leading yourself and others. So what does it mean to trust yourself, including the parts of you that may be hard to trust?

The practice of trusting yourself, and supporting others in trusting themselves fully, involves acknowledging and giving space to all parts and versions of yourself—from the past, present, and future. It also involves integrating lessons from the past and staying open to what the world has to teach you now. For instance, you may tend to reject or act harshly toward parts of yourself that were protective in an earlier period of your life.

When you model openness, trust, and vulnerability, while staying connected to your body, **you signal that it is safe for others to do the same.**

As a young person, Julie learned that showing up as tough, as having it all together, and as not needing any help was the safest and most useful way to be. As her context changed and she developed healthy adult relationships, this tendency got in the way of connecting more deeply in important relationships. Facing a significant health crisis forced Julie to surrender to her humanness, to accept and even ask for help. She shared: "Although I felt uncomfortable to stretch in this way, I also felt amazing as I reevaluated my way of relating across contexts. Learning how to give space and show up with more vulnerability in relationships, then trusting that others would meet that vulnerability with care, was a real growth point for me. The more protective part of me, however, continues to serve in contexts that are not safe. And sometimes I am disappointed and wonder, 'Is showing up in this way worth it?'" There are no guarantees even with embodied presence. Growth, connection, and a meaningful life ask that we all take risks. And sometimes we get hurt along the way.

Trusting yourself involves acknowledging the insights and wisdom that your body communicates to you in any given moment. When in self-doubt, you may find yourself adapting and transforming to whatever the context is calling for, rather than grounding into your full self. This is not only exhausting but destabilizing. You may feel lost and disconnected from yourself.

Trust is also a relational experience. As a leader, you regularly signal to those around you whether you trust them, whether they can trust you, and whether your shared culture is grounded in trust. As humans, we are continuously sending and receiving cues of safety.

Remember, trust is a felt experience. Reflect for a moment on how it feels as someone you are familiar with approaches you—they are making eye contact, smiling, moving calmly toward you with attentiveness. Now imagine how it feels as that same person is walking toward you with a flat expression on their face and not making eye contact. In which scenario do you feel safer? The first provides cues of safety; the second may trigger in you the sense that something is wrong.

Cues of safety (and danger) extend beyond individuals. Trust is also part of our organizational cultures, and you can influence trust at that level through your leadership. When you model openness, trust, and vulnerability, and can stay connected to your body and yourself, you signal to those around you that it is safe for them to do the same. It is true that organizational cultures do not change overnight, and are heavily influenced by values, attitudes, and behaviors of senior leaders; at the same time, cultures are made up of people, and everyone has a role to play in shifting the narrative.

We believe that the most important thing you can do as a leader to shift a culture is to be your true, authentic self.

We also believe that a huge part of trusting yourself is developing a greater awareness of the sensations you feel in your body (interoceptive awareness), learning how to get curious about the sensations and to investigate what they might be telling you. Although your life experiences have generated biases that may blur the signals, when your body is on board, and you can tune in to body sensations with genuine curiosity and openness, a lot can be learned.

Casey has guided thousands of people through an exercise that taps into trust, called the BODY Acronym Exercise. This tool emerged through the development of her TEDx Talk. The exercise, which you will find at the end of this pillar, allows a step-by-step process to unfold, to help you pay attention to your body's wisdom and act in alignment with it.

The BODY Acronym, in short, is:

- Breathe
- Observe
- Delay
- say Yes

Casey reported that most folks find the first two steps of the exercise easier to practice than the last two. She has noticed that most people, when guided, can easily bring awareness to their *breathing*, and allow their breath to naturally deepen. They can *observe* physical sensations in their body, like tightness, tingling, pulsing, heat, cold. But when it's time to *delay*—or create more space around the sensations they feel so that deeper wisdom can be revealed—resistance often arises, especially when what they feel are more uncomfortable sensations. Some people truly want to squirm out of their seat rather than pay attention to uncomfortable sensations in their body. This is completely normal, especially for a person with unhealed trauma.

When practiced safely and consistently, though, people can build mastery around sitting with various sensations within themselves without so much reactivity. When this happens, they inevitably realize that their body is asking for something or offering up wisdom to get their needs met. When they say *yes* to that wisdom—when it is honored, acted upon, and celebrated—self-trust ensues.

Every time you choose to say yes to yourself and your body's wisdom, and then act in alignment, you give yourself the gift of stronger self-trust. This act is easier when your body wisdom sounds something like "I'm cold, put a sweater on me" than when your body wisdom asks you to have that hard conversation, even though you hate conflict; to get out of that relationship, even though you've invested fifteen years into it; or to move your family across the country, even though you don't know how it will unfold. Those yeses tend to be much, much more difficult to act upon.

Why Integration Matters

As a leader, you are often asked to "execute." While this word may now be defined as "to carry out, to perform, or to put into effect," in its origin "to execute" means "to judge, to decide, to choose, to cut off, or to limit options." When you lead yourself to do your work in the world, you need to be discerning about what options you limit in order to preserve your energy, develop patterns to build your energy, and align your energy with your most important mission. As you become more whole and begin to live in a state of integrity with yourself, your vision and goals have an opportunity to become clearer. As a result, executing in alignment becomes easier.

Part of the practice of integration involves showing up as the same "you" in all parts of your life. Being yourself in all contexts can be terrifying and freeing at the same time. It requires vulnerability, and the willingness to hold space for yourself and the sensations that arise in your body. According to Sōtō Zen monk and teacher Shunryū Suzuki, staying on this path requires us to acknowledge that "each of you is perfect the way you are . . . and you can use a little improvement."

In the past, it was expected that a person would carve out different personas and not bring their whole self to work. There is now a lot more openness within work culture toward greater authenticity. Boundaries continue to be important, and different professional contexts have their own specific requirements. At the same time, when you show up as your whole self within the work context, you help others relate better to you, and that leads to better outcomes.

Consider for a moment the cost of not living and leading as your integrated self. How much energy in your system is depleted by masking and hiding important parts of you? How much effort has to be put toward maintaining both a work self and a home self? What if this wasn't the case? Where might you direct the energy and focus you would reclaim by simply living and leading as your integrated self?

> You cannot fully be
> yourself if you can't accept
> or trust parts of yourself.

Work-life balance versus work-life integration

You may wonder at this point how showing up as your full, integrated self might affect work-life balance. Although finding an equilibrium between your personal and work lives may be an important goal, this concept has its limitations. We argue that compartmentalizing these parts of our lives does not encourage flexibility or living in alignment. Integration, in contrast, creates a greater sense of safety and attunement to yourself and others around you, which facilitates your ability to use the wisdom of your mind-body better.

Work-life integration invites you to behave in alignment across the different areas of your life. As Julie experienced more work-life integration, she found herself dressing more similarly across different domains of her life, arranging her spaces in ways that she liked and that supported her body, whether at work or at home, and no longer hiding important ways of being. "For instance," Julie shared, "I will often sit on the floor, stand, or squat rather than sit in a chair—and usually some combination of all of these positions. I don't apologize for needing to move my body, nourish my body, or take care of my body." Dalila described this evolving need for congruence as the need to "cross-pollinate" who we are across all domains of our life, reminding ourselves that when we act in incongruent ways, we compromise our beliefs and who we are through our behaviors.

Over the course of the past few years, you may, like many of us, have experienced a blurring of boundaries between work and personal life. Maybe your organization is still figuring out hybrid work, and you flip from wearing a suit one day to having your dog sit in on your management meeting the next. This moment in time is a natural experiment, during which we are navigating an ever-evolving reality.

- Has this made you feel more comfortable being more "yourself" at work?

- Have you felt more empathy for, and trust in, your colleagues, who have also let their guards down and shown more of their true selves?

- Or perhaps you have experienced a greater sense of disconnection from your colleagues with increased distance from them?

- Have you found it more difficult as a leader to engage with your staff, who have been managing their attention flexibly in order to meet both home and work demands and maintain their well-being?

- What can you take away from this experience that will be valuable to you in showing up as your integrated self moving forward?

Even before the recent move to increased remote work, the evolution toward more flexible work arrangements was well underway. One of the leaders we spoke with told us that her team is all over the world. She spoke of how challenging it is to feel a sense of connection with them and to support them in feeling safe and able to do good work. To create closeness and safety, and to promote a shared sense of compassion and support for one another, she encourages her team to connect about things in their lives that are not directly related to work. This is meant to give everyone a felt sense of others' realities, which often turn out to mirror their own.

Trust, Integration, and Leadership

Trust is a prerequisite for becoming a more integrated version of yourself, while also creating integrated and cohesive teams, work cultures, and collective growth.

You can overcome the psychological constraints arising from your fears of not being enough—good enough, smart enough, fast enough, etcetera—and trust that you *are* enough and can get your own needs met. This process calls on you to open yourself up to the possibility of seeing how your strengths, and who you are as a whole unique individual, can contribute to the world around you.

You cannot fully be yourself if there are parts of you that you can't accept or trust. And if you purposely leave part of you out, your mind-body will sense this lack of cohesion and keep you in the cycle of fear, control, and distrust. How can you expect others to trust you, and how can you create work cultures grounded in trust, if you do not trust yourself?

When you show up in an integrated, cohesive fashion, others around you will sense that cohesiveness and be attracted to it. When you trust others and others trust you, you can create amazing teams, and connect in transformative ways with people and ideas.

Exercises to Bring Your Body on Board

Try the BODY Acronym exercise

Remember, the acronym stands for:

- Breathe
- Observe
- Delay
- say Yes

Bring yourself to a comfortable position, either sitting or lying down. If it feels safe for you, close your eyes.

Begin to attune to your breath, noticing the expansion on the inhale and the contraction on the exhale. Allow your breath to help your nervous system settle. Take five to ten breaths, or more.

Scan your body for sensations—tension, tightness, tingling, openness, and so on. Observe what you feel and where you feel it. What sensation is most asking for your awareness? In other words, where is your body's voice the loudest or most prominent? Let your awareness focus there.

Delay. Don't fix it; just feel it. Imagine that there is a curious explorer inside you examining the sensation with compassion. What else do you notice about it? Is it dark or light? Dense or diffuse? Big or small?

Where does the sensation start? How long has it been there? Notice what arises as you spend some time with the sensation and your mind-body.

Eventually, ask the sensation, "What wisdom are you trying to communicate? What do you need?" Be with the question.

The wisdom you receive may be telling you to attend to the physical in a tactical way, such as by putting on a sweater or stretching, or the wisdom may be more profound. Don't judge it. Trust it.

Say yes to that wisdom and offer your mind-body what you need. Act on the message you received.

Trust that your body knows how to dance

Find a space where you can move comfortably, away from talking and other distractions. Turn off your phone.

Ensure a present state of mind without intoxicants. This is not a "drink in hand" kind of dance party! Dress comfortably and consider going barefoot to connect more to the energy of your body.

Choose some music. Perhaps dim the lights. Consider diffusing essential oils or lighting a candle.

Play your music, however loudly or softly, whatever calls to you.

Allow yourself to move to the music. You may wish to close your eyes and start with slower movements. Move part of your body and feel it. Perhaps rocking from foot to foot with the beat.

There is no right way to do this. Let the music move you.

Practice to "remember"

Commit to a daily embodiment practice, whether it be meditation, yoga, walking, dance, or another form of movement. Trust that through the consistency of the practice, you are building your resilience and your capacity to "remember," or reconnect to, the core of yourself.

Know that this resilience is at the heart of your ability to lead from a place of integration, and to hold space for great things to happen.

Consistency is the key, and the practice need not be long.

Finding Purpose and Contribution

Clarity of purpose can find you over time, when you're ready and open in your body to receive it.

WHEN COURTNEY SPOKE to Darshan, a retired senior executive, about his leadership journey, he became very contemplative. "As a leader, I always had a view of helping my team members learn more about themselves," he said. Darshan explained that, with over three decades of public and private sector experience, he came to see work and leadership as a platform, or a practice, for developing himself and others. "As a leader, you are helping people develop their full potential through their work," he shared.

When asked to define embodied leadership, Darshan quite easily distilled it down to its essence: "As an Embodied Leader, you are centered in your values and principles. Your leadership flows out of you naturally. You are not relying on tools or tricks—whatever you do, it's really you." He said that when leaders operate from that place of centeredness, of integration, of integrity, people notice and seek them out. "Embodied Leaders are not acting; they are just being. Only when you develop this inner sense of yourself, of being centered within yourself, can you impart that feeling to other people as well."

While Darshan may have had a propensity toward embodied leadership given a background in contemplative traditions and a lifelong orientation toward service and citizenship, that does not mean that the transition to the Integrator style was an easy one. Throughout his long career, Darshan met with many personal and professional challenges, but he maintained a growth mindset that allowed him to see these challenges as opportunities for self-development. "Crisis brings you to your knees, and creates an opening for deeper exploration," he said. "The real issue is, Who am I and what do I want to do with the only life that I have?"

This pillar is about tapping into your body's wisdom to clarify your purpose and guide you in making your most important contributions. If you feel stuck doing what others think you should be doing in life and in leadership, at this point in the journey you may be starting to feel a bit of conflict with that outward expectation. Or maybe, like Darshan, you have been brought to your knees so many times that the cracks have turned into large crevices, creating incredible space for deeper exploration. In this pillar, you will capitalize on the openings that have been created thus far, allowing you to break through and find the fulfillment and expansion that comes from being clear on your own purpose, and making meaningful contributions through life and leadership.

Who Do You Want to Be When You Grow Up?

Not too long ago, while discussing her career goals with her manager, Courtney was asked, "Where do you see yourself in five years, ten years?" She received this as a pretty standard question, one she has posed to her staff many times.

Her answer was less about a place or a job and more about a state of being. She said, "I want to be more centered in myself, more authentic in my leadership, able to take on more responsibilities from a place of resilience, confidence, and abundance, and make an impact through living in alignment with my deeper purpose and contribution." It wasn't the standard answer, but it was a truthful answer—one that has guided her more over the past few years than vying for a specific job or working for a specific organization. Even now, this answer still resonates deeply in her body.

You may be thinking that working toward a state of being is a difficult pitch in our performance-oriented world, where we are rewarded for results and getting stuff done. You, too, likely spend or have spent quite a bit of time "doing" and have received praise for how much you can accomplish.

But if you are "doing" without a clear sense of purpose; if you are doing what you think you "should" rather than what's truly aligned; if you are not paying attention to your mind-body and who you are being; and if you are saying yes to what does not serve you, not only will you eventually feel dull, stuck, and unfulfilled, but you'll also hit an upper ceiling on your capacity to be an influential leader.

At some point, you need to focus less on "doing" and more on "being." What does this involve? It requires a shift from thinking to sensing, and a shift from managing to leading, specifically in an embodied way.

Great leaders who lead with power and purpose move beyond putting check marks in boxes. Great leaders, in our opinion, lead by leveraging their bodies as somatic copilots, and by embracing their bodies' purpose-driven wisdom for growth and impact. When you stay committed to the journey of the Embodied Leader, you get clearer on your purpose and contribution, you develop passion and perseverance for that purpose, or what psychologist Angela Duckworth calls "grit," and you become the fulfilled and impactful person you've always known yourself to be.

Your Body as Your Purpose Guide

At this point in the book, maybe you've realized where in your life and leadership you feel contracted or misaligned—where you feel a sense of anxiety or depression, illness or burnout, or simply an uncomfortable ache for more. Maybe you've also realized where in your life and leadership you feel expanded—where you feel a sense of flow, excitement, or ease. Remember, contraction and expansion in your body can inform you about what to do next. These sensations, when seen as guideposts on your journey, can lead you toward a greater sense of purpose or contribution.

Julie was experiencing a misalignment with the organization she was working for that only grew. In the beginning, her gut told her that the new job was not a great fit, but she convinced herself that she could make it work. And she did, to some extent, but at a significant cost to her well-being. She remarked, "At one period during my years working for this organization, I was practicing yoga for 1.5 hours or more a day, every day, just to be able to show up in a semi-present way in my life." Eventually, she left this organization to build a work life that is more wholly in alignment with her purpose and contribution. "The journey has been scary and invigorating," she shared. Initially, she did not know what her work life would look like, but she did know that her entire body was screaming an expansive *yes* to this next step. Thus far in her life, she can honestly say that it has been one of her best career decisions.

As you move along the Embodied Leader path, you will become more and more attuned to the types of sensations described above, and you will gain the confidence and courage to listen and act on their wisdom. Your purpose comes from within, and when your body is on board, you can attune to those feelings to further align yourself to your purpose.

In *Reboot: Leadership and the Art of Growing Up*, entrepreneur and professional coach Jerry Colonna recounts his personal awakening at a time in his life when, from the outside, he had all the money he needed and massive success as a venture capitalist, but he was deeply unhappy. Outer results without inner alignment leads to a state of contraction. He needed to change to become the kind of adult and leader he wanted to be.

Where have you felt an awakening to the power of embodiment through engaging with the exercises in this book so far? In what ways have you felt more aware, attuned to your mind-body, courageous, connected, and trusting of yourself and others?

Does this newfound embodiment have you asking deeper questions of yourself, such as:

- Who am I, really?
- What am I here to do?
- How am I truly meant to lead?

We hope so.

Embodiment facilitates meaning, and the guidance that arrives as you practice it supports purposeful decision-making and deeper self-discovery that can help you answer these questions.

Find Your Deeper Purpose

So how do you find more clarity around your purpose?

At the end of June in 2014, Casey had been traveling through Southeast Asia with a dear friend for about five and a half weeks. Through a series of synchronistic events, they found themselves—for the last five days of their trip—in the jungle at a silent retreat center a few hours outside Bali. The silence combined with the knowing that Casey would soon return home, triggered a head spin of big questions related to her work and life: "Should I quit my job? Should I get a new one? Should I double down on business? Ditch them both? Go back to school? What am I meant to do next?"

Later, while out on a long walk, she heard herself ask something much deeper—the real question she wanted an answer to "What is my dharma? My purpose? My true contribution?" She took that question into the twice daily yoga and meditation practices, wrote about it in her journal, and walked the on-site labyrinth with it in mind.

Then one evening, while in a facilitated meditation, she received the wisdom that offered all the clarity she needed. Casey described the illuminating moment: "I was guided on

a journey through my body, being invited to bring awareness to different parts, from my lower limbs and the base of
my spine upward. By the time my awareness arrived at my
heart space, I could feel my breath expand me effortlessly
in all directions, and a warmth washed over me. My eyes
instantly began to well up with tears. And then I heard these
words: 'Your purpose is love.' It was not what I expected, but
it felt exactly right."

The next day, she put pen to paper and wrote in her
journal: "If my purpose is love, what do I do next?" And
without skipping a beat, she answered that question.

When she returned home, she led her life in a different
direction, with courage and confidence. She quit her job,
journeyed into her business full-time, committed to practices that helped her embody love, and became anchored in
bringing love to others.

Casey's unwavering trust in the truth of her own body's
wisdom helped her take the leap she needed in her work,
and everything worked out, almost effortlessly. In her experience, that's what can happen when we act in alignment
with deeper purpose. To this day, she acknowledges her
truth. She knows that her contribution in life and leadership
is love. The expression of that love changes as she changes,
but it remains something that she can stay grounded in,
especially when moments get confusing and hard.

Defining your purpose or reason for being doesn't have
to feel like a huge and untouchable task. Though clarity of
purpose can arrive in a moment like a lightning strike, it
is perhaps more likely to unfold over time through attuning to your mind-body as you live each moment. In other

words, you absolutely don't have to go away to a foreign country and spend days in silence to find clarity of purpose or realize where you're meant to contribute. Clarity of purpose can find you over time, when you're ready and open in your body to receive it. When asked about clarity of purpose, Darshan shared, "It is already within you. All of this already exists within you. Everyone that you work with, especially in a leadership role, is a mirror for you. If you pay attention, you will see your purpose reflected back to you."

When you pay attention, you are more likely to notice moment-to-moment callings and opportunities for contribution.

These moment-to-moment callings are typically experienced as expansion in the body, because they are resonating with the purpose that is already within you. Casey feels open, uplifted, excited, and even feels chills—she calls them "truth tingles"—when she's onto something. Her body gives her clues about what next step to take, and she believes that it is following these clues, like bread crumbs, that eventually connects her to where and how she is meant to contribute next. Since her profound experience in 2014, her body has guided her to let go of working as a dietitian and yoga teacher, and to embrace supporting others whose purpose is evolving as a coach and embodiment guide. It also guided her to write, speak, teach, and tell stories about the challenges and gifts of the purpose-driven path.

Where to Begin

Asking the question "What is my purpose?" is a great place to start, and staying committed to your embodiment practices is key to supporting you in this process. We also want to offer you a few other, more precise practices to support your discovery.

Track when you feel most expansive

Track in your current life and leadership when you feel most expansive and in flow. Even if you feel like you're not fully on your path, chances are you get glimpses of your true purpose in many micro moments. Like a magnet, the purpose that is in you attracts what resonates with it. Your purpose pulls opportunities toward you whether you're aware of it or not. It's time to mine for those moments.

One way to do this is to notice and tap into what we call embodied markers. We've already mentioned the importance of noticing feelings of expansion and contraction, as well as other bodily responses such as chills or goose bumps. Other embodied markers could include feeling a deep level of engagement when undertaking certain activities, for instance when you provide a team member with heartfelt, honest feedback on their performance; or you might feel energized after a certain type of experience, such as presenting work that is really meaningful to you to a receptive audience. Flow, which we mentioned in Pillars 2 and 4, is also an excellent embodied marker of whether what you are doing is well aligned with your purpose and contribution. If you are unfamiliar with flow, think of it as a state of maximum focus, engagement, and enjoyment, where you are pursuing an adequate level of challenge and receiving immediate feedback on how you are doing, from yourself or others. For instance, Courtney feels most in flow when she is completely immersed in the act of writing, when she is clear in her mind and her ideas are flowing easily, and when she loses a sense of time.

Only you can decide to be all in. **When you, your mind-body, and your purpose align, it's like an instrument coming into tune.**

Whether you tap into the sensation of expansion or contraction, truth tingles, engagement, energy, or flow, the key is building a practice of noticing and tracking these different markers as clues to whether you are on the best path, or whether you have veered off course. For instance, in that meeting where you were presenting your ideas to the group, what did you feel in your body before, during, and after the presentation? On a scale from 1 to 10, how much expansion did you feel at each stage? When you were working with a specific client one-on-one, when did your body feel most energized and engaged? How different did your body feel when working directly with the client versus note-taking or documenting afterward?

When you go through your day as it is right now and track where you feel most engaged, energetic, and expansive, and where you are in a state of flow, you'll receive clues about what brings you joy. And joy is an important element of purpose.

Look for joy

Look for joy in the past to offer clues about present and future joy. Reflecting on moments throughout your life when you were absolutely at your best can offer clues about when you feel the most on purpose.

When Casey is leading workshops around purpose for her clients, she asks them to close their eyes and take a breath. She guides them to remember a specific moment when they were a child, a moment when they got lost in time, when they experienced complete flow, or when they were in their joy or expansion. Then she leads her clients to embody that version of themselves—to become that child for a moment. She encourages them to not judge the first memory that comes to mind. They typically do; it's only natural. They typically feel like each of their memories is "nothing significant" until they realize they are about to unlock something about their natural gifts and tendencies from their memories.

One client remembered reading cuddled up in bed, not wanting any family members to know she was awake as she got lost in a novel. She remembered reading a specific type of book, one with strong female protagonists paving their own path. Another client recalled sitting on the bathroom counter cross-legged as a kid, playing with mirrors. They got lost in seeing many different versions of their own face. They could sit there for hours, moving the mirrors to create a kaleidoscope effect—like they were creating alternate realities all at once. Another instantly remembered sitting near a river at their grandmother's house, trying to catch tadpoles. They were talking to rocks, feeling the water run over their feet, and forgetting to come in for lunch when it was time.

Casey commented: "As I watch my clients relive their childhood joys, their bodies immediately shift—they open up, shoulders drop back, a smile returns to their face, sometimes a tear trickles down. They experience something so true, so real, about their natural essence, without fully realizing it."

They repeat this exercise twice more, dropping into different moments when they were older. Casey invites them to tell her about another moment in life when they were pulsing, absolutely at their best. That kicks off another round of sharing.

The client who loved reading books with strong female protagonists also felt at her best speaking on a stage with hundreds of people in the audience whose attention she could hold with power and purpose. When she speaks, she feels most authentic—she becomes the leader she read about as a child. She is seen. She connects. She creates impact. This client also told Casey about feeling in flow when she quit her job with confidence.

After digging into the depths with these clients, threads of truth are illuminated and they expand into who they really are and what they are really here for. They have an embodied response to this "remembering." What they naturally do underneath what they do becomes crystal clear. And they are empowered to apply that special gift to not just their work but to their life and leadership as an integrated experience.

What about you? Take a breath and remember a specific moment when you were a kid, got lost in time, and experienced flow or expansion. What comes up for you?

Own Your Purpose and Be All In

In his book *The Great Work of Your Life*, Stephen Cope brilliantly translates an ancient text about dharma—which refers to vocation, purpose, or calling—and makes it meaningful for modern-day times. He shared, "First, look to your *dharma,* then, do it full out!" When you imbue your purpose into everything you do—when you do it full out—your actions become even more valuable. In the context of work and leadership, it becomes part of how you create deeper, richer, and more transformational experiences for yourself and all the people who cross your path directly or indirectly. When you give yourself even more permission to own your purpose, you also feel more fulfilled and alive. As one of the leaders we spoke to put it, "When I started, it was about getting it all done, but throughout the years, I have come to realize, and tune in to, what really inspires me."

Darshan spoke of leadership as service and said that service comes from a place of caring and love for others: "In order to lead them, you have to love them. And out of that love comes a sense of service." One of the ways that leaders serve others is by helping them make their most valuable contribution. Darshan believes that we all have a responsibility to make our contribution. "We are here to serve creation as a whole. We are obliged to do our part. Everything is connected, and everything matters, no matter how small. Even small things can make a big difference." And when people are empowered to contribute, it has a ripple effect. "Making your contribution adds to your being. You feel empowered. It affects your work, your home life, your communities," Darshan said. When we each do our work in the world, it benefits everyone.

We are all leaders in our own lives. If you are reading this from the vantage point of a parent, you play an important leadership role in fostering the well-being, development, and satisfaction of your family. If you are an entrepreneur, you know how important your leadership skills are to driving yourself and your business toward success. If you are a manager or organizational leader, people in your team and across the organization look to you for clear direction, guidance, and recognition. If you are in a body, like the rest of us, you are also a leader to yourself—setting your personal goals, reflecting on your challenges and successes, and guiding yourself through the journey of your life.

As a leader, it is your responsibility to be clear in your own purpose and direction and to integrate all elements of yourself into your practice of leadership. Only you can decide to be all in. When you, your mind-body, and your purpose align, it's like an instrument coming into tune. And when you hear the sound of that finely tuned instrument, you will feel it in your body, and those around you will feel it too. As Darshan put it, "When you go beneath the intellectual, from the head to the heart and the gut, that's when you know what it means to be a leader."

If you are in a body, you are also a leader to yourself, guiding yourself through the journey of life.

The exercises outlined below will support you in clarifying your purpose, being laser focused in your direction and actions, and drawing on your body's wisdom to navigate and course correct as you make your most meaningful contributions.

During his interview, Darshan reminded us that we can learn from everyone: "Everyone that you work with, especially in a leadership role, is your teacher." What you learn you can either reject or integrate. He also highlighted that embodied leadership is not the norm, but when you see it, you recognize it, and having more of those people in your life can help you to develop into the leader you want to be. "Finding role models, and being associated with them, is one of the greatest blessings in life. They become a source of nurturing for you." Darshan emphasized that the journey of embodied leadership is lonely without a lot of role models. By engaging in this journey, you are becoming a model for others in your life and leadership. You are realizing the infinite possibilities in yourself, and helping others see the infinite possibilities in themselves. So don't be shy. Share your story, reflections, and gifts with others, so that we all may benefit.

Exercises to Bring Your Body on Board

Identify your purpose
Close your eyes and consider the following questions. You may find it helpful to write your reflections/responses in a journal after imaging them.

What am I here to do?

Who do I want to become?

What is my purpose, and what do I envision for my future to live this out most fully?

Write without attention to grammar, spelling, or style. Let your ideas flow freely.

Use your body as your purpose guide
As you move along the Embodied Leader path, you will become increasingly attuned to your body's signals and sensations, and you will be able to use this information to guide your actions.

Your body will tell you when you are outside your purpose (feeling of contraction) or aligned with your purpose (feeling of expansion). This awareness will allow you to say no to what does not align with your purpose and to avoid detours.

Start by paying attention to the level of energy, engagement, and expansion you feel from various tasks or experiences during your day.

Reflect on your experiences. For instance: How did it feel to manage that meeting? How did it feel to work with that client one-on-one?

You may also get insights from thinking about the past. What were you doing when you felt the most engaged, the most committed, the most expansive? When were you at your absolute best? When were you in flow? What were you doing when you felt most authentic?

Begin to notice tasks or experiences that are draining, when you feel disengaged and contracted. By tracking these moments, you will receive clues about what brings you joy and what doesn't. Interestingly, what brings you joy may not always correlate with what you are best at, what you've been trained for, or what you get paid for.

Your purpose is what you are doing when you are living in alignment with the most authentic, integrated, and embodied version of you. Others will benefit when you are on purpose, and your body can help you zero in on what you are most meant to do.

As you engage in your day, tune in to your body and listen for your somatic copilot's signals. Your body will show you the way.

Envision your future integrated self

Block off ten to twenty minutes. Find a comfortable position, seated or otherwise, and ground into your body.

You have the capacity to drop into a future version of you, ten or twenty years in the future, a you that is more embodied and has more deeply integrated wisdom from your life experiences. Who is this person? What qualities do they embody? How do they show up for life and leadership? How do they use body wisdom to navigate and course correct? What difference do they make or have they made in the world? Imagine a question that you can ask this future version of you. A question that can help guide you today.

Notice the sensations in your body as you imagine the answers to these questions, and allow those sensations to refine and focus this image of your future integrated self. Know that this version of you is already inside you.

Leading with
Your Whole Self

We are most effective when we work together, engaging in levels of collaboration that are only possible when we are truly present.

EMBODIED LEADERS ARE needed now. There are many doors to embodiment; the result is leading from a place of authenticity, curiosity, empathy, compassion, and alignment. In October 2022, at the Ottawa International Writers Festival, when Gabor Maté was asked what one thing we could all do that would have the greatest effect on the toxic culture we are living in, his response was "Get to know oneself." He said that "when you are authentic, you do not behave in toxic ways."

If this book has helped you bring your body on board, and moved you to a greater embodied presence in your life and leadership, then our purpose has been accomplished. What comes next is how you will maintain and further grow that embodiment into your future. How will you notice the Explorer, Connector, or Integrator in you, and how will you use that knowledge to continue to grow? As your context, life, and body changes, you will continue to evolve. Doing so from a place of embodied presence will facilitate living life to your fullest potential.

The journey to embodied leadership is a one-way ticket, but definitely not a straight line. Once you have connected to yourself in this deep, integrated way, going back feels impossible. And, in fact, it is impossible. But that does not mean that embodied leadership becomes easy or risk free. Meeting yourself where you are can be scary. Vulnerability is key to living a meaningful life, and it can be painfully hard. Honoring body wisdom often goes against expectations. Staying connected with yourself and others when things get hot or challenging requires resilience. It also requires support. Key to building that support is sharing about your journey. This human experience, this leadership experience, is not solitary; it happens in community.

To support this path, we invite you to ask yourself this: Do I want to keep drifting along with only a few of my senses guiding me, or do I want to live full out? This is not a question you ask yourself once but over and over again. You now know that greater levels of satisfaction, connection, engagement, purpose, and meaning are possible; and you know that embodiment is essential to reaching this way of being. Now that you are on the Embodied Leader path, we offer you three main actions to focus on as you continue your journey: practice, reflect, and connect. These three actions are of equal importance, and you may find it helpful to envision them as a three-legged stool, each leg supporting the stool so it can stand.

Practice

As you have experienced in this book, embodiment can be developed. Each cycle of life led with embodiment brings more breadth and depth of understanding, experience, and presence. The more you practice being present to your mind-body, your feelings, and your sensations, the greater your capacity for embodiment and for embodied leadership.

We hope that the exercises presented throughout the book have supported you along your journey. The key to getting the most out of these exercises is to make them personal, to practice them with consistency, and to integrate them into your life. As you explore and experiment with these exercises, you will discover those that most resonate with you, and you will be able to make them your own. Consistency is more important than variety or amount of time when it comes to cultivating a more direct connection with your mind-body and building a relationship with your somatic copilot. It will serve you well to commit to at least one exercise per day to build a solid foundation for your habit. Regularly engaging in your chosen exercises will allow them to become integrated, along with their benefits, into your daily life.

Reflect

At the beginning of this journey, we introduced you to the Embodied Leader styles—Explorer, Connector, Integrator—and invited you to reflect on which style or styles you most identified with. At this stage, we invite you to engage in this reflection again, and to see whether the styles have a different meaning for you. Do you identify differently? What has changed for you?

We also suggested that you keep a journal to take note of observations, reflections, and learnings along the way. If you have done this, we invite you now to take a few minutes to read and reflect on your journal. Questions that can guide your reflection include:

- How have I changed and grown through this journey?
- What has surprised me?
- What is new to me?
- What has shifted in me and in my leadership?
- What are my key takeaways?
- Where would I like to go from here?

If you have not kept a journal, it can be equally helpful to take the opportunity to start one now, and capture the reflections that emerge from the questions above.

As an Embodied Leader,
**you will cultivate courage
and vulnerability in others,
leading from a place of trust.**

Part of the reflection process is also reading and learning from others. If you are already part of a management team, leadership coaching circle, or other supportive group, we encourage you to reflect on your embodiment journey with them. You can also choose a friend with whom you can share your journey and where you would like to take it from here. Reflect with others on what your key takeaways and insights have been. As entrepreneur, leadership coach, and author Yves Doucet reminds his students on a regular basis, sharing what you have learned and the insights you have gained with others is a gift that you are offering them. Be generous with your gifts.

Connect

Connection is so important that it is one of the pillars of this book. We show up as our best, strongest, most authentic self when we consciously connect with ourselves and with others. We are most effective when we work together, engaging in levels of collaboration that are only possible when we are truly present, in our bodies, and attuned to each other. To be present and attuned and to connect requires safety. This is a felt sense and cannot be faked.

As an Embodied Leader, you seek to create environments where this type of connection is possible. Cultures where curiosity and diversity are honored, where people feel included, secure, and safe to be themselves and make their best contributions. Where do you feel this safety and security in your life right now? What environments do not feel safe and secure to you or others, and what can you as a leader do about it? What do you need to do to further grow your competence and courage in this area?

Final Thoughts

Embodiment is about being present in your body and to the world around you. When you drop into awareness of your own inner being, you can lead from a place of inner wisdom. Leading from this place of wisdom brings about greater results for yourself and others, in ways that cut through the noise, stress, and feelings of overwhelm. When you are in tune with your body and your environment, you can find and create safety, security, and the change that is needed to support others in tuning in to themselves, especially when things get uncomfortable.

As an Embodied Leader, you will cultivate courage and vulnerability in others, leading from a place of trust. Through your example, we know that many others will be inspired to follow in your footsteps on this path to purpose and contribution.

One more exercise to bring your body on board

As a final exercise, we invite you to share your story, so that it can support and guide others on their Embodied Leader path. Depending on your personality, you may do this through intimate one-on-one conversations, speaking on a stage, or something in between.

In what way can you share what you know, so that there are more Embodied Leaders in the world growing resilience, nurturing connection, and finding deeper purpose?

REMEMBER, THIS journey is a process, not a destination or outcome. It is the process of coming back to yourself.

Yoga teacher, physical therapist, and author Judith Hanson Lasater speaks to the radical shift in perspective that comes with realization: "Nothing outside of you has changed: *you* have changed. And yet, paradoxically, you have *not* changed, but rather have become what you already are. You have just removed the smoke screen of ignorance so that what always had been present has become more apparent."

We are honored to have joined you along your path. We wish for you a rich, purpose-driven, resilient, and joyful life. A life filled with meaningful connections, satisfaction, and impact. With your body on board, you have a way to break the cycle of overwhelm, and be the leader you always knew you could be.

Acknowledgments

From All Three of Us:

To the Page Two team, thank you for your encouragement, guidance, and belief in us and this book. Special thanks to our editor, Kendra Ward, who skillfully challenged and helped polish our ideas, without losing the essence of our voice.

To the amazing leaders who shared their stories with us, thank you for your courage, vulnerability, and willingness to share your journey with others. We hope that we have done justice to your well-lived experiences.

From Courtney:

I am grateful to the strong, courageous, vulnerable leaders I have the privilege to know in my life. The ones who are not afraid to show that they are fully human, and who encourage, guide, and mentor others to do the same.

To my many colleagues, thank you for your trust, your generosity, and your willingness to truly connect. It is an honor to pursue shared goals with you.

To my yoga students, thank you for showing up on the mat every week, and for creating a safe space for us all to relearn how to be in our bodies, and connect to our true selves.

Thank you to the many volunteers who tested our materials, read early drafts, and listened to me talk about this book. Special thanks to Roberte Richard, Brigitte Lajoie, Gordana Krcevinac, Tariq Bhatti, Yves Doucet, Prem Robin Campbell, Kelly Bannister, Vish Chatterji, and Yves Pelletier. Your advice, wisdom, guidance, and heartfelt encouragement kept us on track and motivated to reach the finish line.

Julie and Casey—thank you for entertaining this crazy idea when I first mentioned it to each of you in December 2019. Who knew what we were getting ourselves into. It has been a pleasure to be on this journey with you both.

Thank you to my close friends and family—including my sisters Julie and Kelly, and their families—for their unwavering support. Mom and Dad, I wish I could have seen you hold a copy of the book. Your wisdom, warmth, and humor are with me every day.

To my husband and best friend, Glen K. Amo—it is on the foundation of your love, trust, and belief in me that I become more and more myself. I love you. Meu.

From Julie:

Gratitude to my teachers and healers. Thank you for showing me the importance of authenticity and guiding me back to trusting in my own embodied experience.

To my clients, who have shown up courageously and taught me at least as much as I hope to have taught them.

To my cherished inner circle. My journey toward deepening embodiment has been supported greatly by your loving presence.

To many who shared feedback and insights along this journey. Special thanks to Van Mardian and Bruce Hutchison for providing feedback on an early draft.

Casey and Courtney, I cannot imagine a more beautiful co-writing experience.

To the trees, water, and nature, for your constant regulating presence.

From Casey:

I'd like to thank my parents, Jack and Terry, and siblings, Blake, Jarid, and Jody, for supporting my journey into embodied leadership through entrepreneurship. I have never doubted your trust or support for the unconventional path I chose—one rich with lessons and stories, including some that made it into this book.

Thank you to my dear friends who read early copies, cooked dinner while I wrote, and offered honest feedback at various stages of the process. And to the ones who have supported me and helped me co-regulate through especially difficult moments. It is the greatest gift to do life and leadership together.

To those incredible leaders who offered their knowledge, wisdom, and experiences early on in the process—Tahira Benjamin, Erica Courdae, Lindsay Austin, Christy Harrison, Leah Skerry, Gabriel William, and Tony Loria—thank you!

I am grateful to my clients, who offer up so much wisdom and truth through our work and who trust me to guide them into their bodies and hold space for whatever they find there. I appreciate you more than you'll ever know.

Thank you to the wisdom of yoga—my first embodiment teacher, and then to the healers, mentors, guides, bodyworkers, academics, and everyday people with whom I've studied.

And of course, Julie and Courtney, thank you for showing me how beautiful a co-writing collaboration could be. You both constantly blow me away with your wisdom, gifts, talent, and trust. We couldn't do this without each other. I love you!

Notes

Lead from the Inside Out

"the mind is distracted." Willa Blythe Baker, *The Wakeful Body: Somatic Mindfulness as a Path to Freedom* (Boulder, CO: Shambhala Publications, 2021).

Your ability to thrive depends in part. Arianna Huffington, *Thrive: The Third Metric to Redefining Success and Creating a Life of Well-Being, Wisdom and Wonder* (New York: Harmony, 2015).

Our bodies are deprived of fundamental needs. Cal Newport, *Digital Minimalism: Choosing a Focused Life in a Noisy World* (New York: Portfolio, 2019).

Guidance for Your Journey

Staying with and creating opportunities for discomfort. K. Woolley and A. Fishbach, "Motivating Personal Growth by Seeking Discomfort," *Psychological Science* 33, no. 4 (April 2022): 510–23.

Pillar 1: Building Body Awareness and Compassion

"awareness of our direct sensory, mental, and emotional experience." Oren Jay Sofer, *Say What You Mean: A Mindful Approach to Nonviolent Communication* (Boulder, CO: Shambhala Publications, 2018).

"the shape of our experience." Richard Strozzi-Heckler,
*The Leadership Dojo: Build Your Foundation as an Exemplary
Leader* (Toronto: Frog Books, 2011).

Julie has developed a practice of tuning into her "felt sense."
In psychology, "felt sense" is a concept that describes when you
are tuned into your body and able to bring your awareness to
what is going on in your body and bodily processes.

describes our core experiences of ourselves as "somatic." Bessel van
der Kolk, *The Body Keeps the Score: Brain, Mind, and Body in the
Healing of Trauma* (New York: Penguin Books, 2015).

"infant's sixth sense." S.W. Porges, "The Infant's Sixth Sense:
Awareness and Regulation of Bodily Processes," *Zero to Three:
Bulletin of the National Center for Clinical Infant Programs* 14
(1993): 12–16.

linked to reduced risk for various health conditions. B. Bonaz,
R.D. Lane, M.L. Oshinsky, P.J. Kenny, R. Sinha, E.A. Mayer, and
H.D. Critchley, "Diseases, Disorders, and Comorbidities of
Interoception," *Trends in Neurosciences* 44, no. 1 (January
2021): 39–51; M.P. Paulus and J.L. Stewart, "Interoception and
Drug Addiction," *Neuropharmacology* 76, part B (January 2014):
342–50; L. Quadt, H.D. Critchley, and S.N. Garfinkel, "The
Neurobiology of Interoception in Health and Disease," *Annals
of the New York Academy of Sciences* 1428, no. 1 (September
2018): 112–28.

"flow states" or being in "the zone." L. Montull, P. Vázquez, L.
Rocas, R. Hristovski, and N. Balagué, "Flow as an Embodied
State: Informed Awareness of Slackline Walking," *Frontiers in
Psychology* 10 (January 2020): 2993.

when faced with real or perceived threats in your environment.
Stephen W. Porges, *Polyvagal Theory: Neurophysiological
Foundations of Emotions, Attachment, Communication,
Self-Regulation* (New York: Norton, 2011).

many of us have become so accustomed to stress that its absence
creates unease. Gabor Maté, *When the Body Says No: The Cost of
Hidden Stress* (Toronto: Vintage Canada, 2004).

you may hear a lot about emotional intelligence. C.R. Seal
    and A. Andrews-Brown, "An Integrative Model of Emotional
    Intelligence: Emotional Ability as a Moderator of the Mediated
    Relationship of Emotional Quotient and Emotional Competence,"
    Organization Management Journal 7 (2010): 143–52.
the related concept of emotional competence. Gabor Maté, *When
    the Body Says No: The Cost of Hidden Stress* (Toronto: Vintage
    Canada, 2004).
Naming or labeling also helps to build awareness. C. Saarni,
    "Emotional Competence: A Developmental Perspective," in R.
    Bar-On and J.D.A. Parker, eds., *The Handbook of Emotional
    Intelligence: Theory, Development, Assessment, and Application
    at Home, School, and in the Workplace* (Hoboken, NJ:
    Jossey-Bass, 2000), 68–91.
their Mindful Self-Compassion approach. Kristin Neff and
    Christopher Germer, *The Mindful Self-Compassion Workbook:
    A Proven Way to Accept Yourself, Build Inner Strength, and
    Thrive* (New York: Guilford Press, 2018).
compassion-focused therapy approach. P. Gilbert, "The Origins
    and Nature of Compassion Focused Therapy," *British Journal of
    Clinical Psychology* 53 (2014): 6–41.
an absence of interpersonal fear. A. Edmondson, "Psychological
    Safety and Learning Behavior in Work Teams," *Administrative
    Science Quarterly* 44, no. 2 (1999): 350–83.
trust within teams. Karen Bluth and Kristin D. Neff, "New Frontiers
    in Understanding the Benefits of Self-Compassion," *Self and
    Identity* 17, no. 6 (2018): 605–8; M. Paakkanen, F. Martela,
    J. Hakanen, et al., "Awakening Compassion in Managers: A
    New Emotional Skills Intervention to Improve Managerial
    Compassion," *Journal of Business and Psychology* 36 (2021):
    1095–1108.
"healing starts by simply becoming mindful." Jack Kornfield,
    "Mindfulness of the Body," n.d., jackkornfield.com/mindfulness
    -of-the-body/.

Pillar 2: Working with Your Mind-Body and Nervous System

neuroplasticity is still present in the aging brain. J. Shaffer, "Neuroplasticity and Clinical Practice: Building Brain Power for Health," *Frontiers in Psychology* 26, no. 7 (July 2016): 1118.

"Story follows state." Deb Dana, *The Polyvagal Theory in Therapy: Engaging the Rhythm of Regulation* (New York: Norton, 2018).

emotion follows physiological changes. William James, *The Principles of Psychology* (1890; repr., New York: Dover, 1950).

where we physically look with our eyes. D. Grand, "Brainspotting a New Brain-Based Psychotherapy Approach," *Trauma and Gewalt* 3 (2011): 276–85.

About 80 percent of the information passing between your body and your brain. Porges, *Polyvagal Theory*.

"any attempt we may make to bypass or ignore." Jill Bolte Taylor, *Whole Brain Living: The Anatomy of Choice and the Four Characters That Drive Our Life* (Carlsbad, CA: Hay House, 2021).

burnout, which leaders around the world are currently experiencing at record levels. Development Dimensions International (DDI) Inc., Global Leadership Forecast 2021, ddiworld.com/global-leadership-forecast-2021.

The vagus nerve is taking center stage these days. S. Breit, A. Kupferberg, G. Rogler, and G. Hasler, "Vagus Nerve as Modulator of the Brain-Gut Axis in Psychiatric and Inflammatory Disorders," *Frontiers in Psychiatry* 9 (2018): 44; Porges, *Polyvagal Theory*.

The autonomic ladder. Dana, *Polyvagal Theory in Therapy*.

Armoring up can also keep positive energy out. Gay Hendricks, *The Big Leap: Conquer Your Hidden Fear and Take Life to the Next Level* (New York: Harper One, 2009).

"window of tolerance." Daniel J. Siegel, *The Developing Mind* (New York: Guilford Press, 1999).

you can reshape and rewire your neural pathways. Norman Doidge, *The Brain That Changes Itself: Stories of Personal Triumph from the Frontiers of Brain Science* (Carlton North, Australia: Scribe Publications, 2010).

"Your ability to observe your own sensations without immediately
reacting to them." Amanda Blake, *Your Body Is Your Brain:
Leverage Your Somatic Intelligence to Find Purpose, Build
Resilience, Deepen Relationships and Lead More Powerfully*
(n.p.: Trokay Press, 2018).

Pillar 3: Taking Risks and Practicing Courage

"Fear is excitement without the breath." Fritz Perls, *Gestalt Therapy
and How It Works* (audiocassette, 1966), quoted in Proper
Psychology, "Fritz Perls: Expand Your Mind—Enlightening
Quotes," YouTube, February 4, 2022, youtube.com/watch?v=BY
6j6J1W6Cg.

"all growth starts at the end of your comfort zone." Team Tony,
"How to Surround Yourself with Good People: 5 Ways to Let Go
of the Relationships That Are Holding You Back," Tony Robbins
website, n.d., tonyrobbins.com/stories/business-mastery/
surround-yourself-with-quality-people/.

you develop an adaptive relationship with stress. S.M. Southwick and
D.S. Charney, "The Science of Resilience: Implications for the
Prevention and Treatment of Depression," *Science* 338, no. 6103
(2012): 79–82.

her powerful TED Talk. Brené Brown, "The Power of Vulnerability,"
video, TED website, December 23, 2010, ted.com/talks/brene_
brown_the_power_of_vulnerability.

"only those who will risk going too far." T.S. Eliot, preface to *Transit
of Venus: Poems*, by Harry Crosby, in *Collected Poems of Harry
Crosby* (Paris: Black Sun Press, 1931), ix.

When you are fearful, you may overestimate risk. S. Wake, J.
Wormwood, and A.B. Satpute, "The Influence of Fear on Risk
Taking: A Meta-analysis," *Cognition and Emotion* 34, no. 6
(September 2020): 1143–59.

unduly biased in how you evaluate information. G. Loewenstein
and J.S. Lerner, "The Role of Emotion in Decision Making," in
The Handbook of Affective Science, ed. R.J. Davidson, H.H.
Goldsmith, and K.R. Scherer (Oxford: Oxford University Press,
2003), 619–42.

"power poses." D.R. Carney, A.J.C. Cuddy, and A.J. Yap, "Power Posing: Brief Nonverbal Displays Affect Neuroendocrine Levels and Risk Tolerance," *Psychological Science* 21, no. 10 (October 2010): 1363–68.

holding more expansive postures can increase testosterone. R.S. Minvaleev, A.D. Nozdrachev, V. Kir'yanova, and A.I. Ivanov, "Postural Influences on the Hormone Level in Healthy Subjects: I. The Cobra Posture and Steroid Hormones," *Human Physiology* 30 (2004): 452–56.

Maslow's hierarchy. A.H. Maslow, "A Theory of Human Motivation," *Psychological Review* 50, no. 4 (1943): 370–96.

finding purpose and fulfillment requires us to take these risks. Scott Barry Kaufman, *Transcend: The New Science of Self-Actualization* (New York: TarcherPerigee, 2020).

There are many excellent resources available. Resmaa Menakem, *My Grandmother's Hands: Racialized Trauma and the Pathway to Mending Our Hearts and Bodies* (Las Vegas: Central Recovery Press, 2017); Bäri A. Williams, *Diversity in the Workplace: Eye-Opening Interviews to Jumpstart Conversations about Identity, Privilege, and Bias* (Emeryville, CA: Rockridge Press, 2020); Ruchika Tulshyan, *Inclusion on Purpose: An Intersectional Approach to Creating a Culture of Belonging at Work* (Cambridge, MA: MIT Press, 2022).

Pillar 4: Consciously Connecting with Yourself and Others

Our brains are wired to be social. Matthew D. Lieberman, *Social: Why Our Brains Are Wired to Connect* (New York: Crown, 2013).

challenge us to reframe our thinking. Bill Burnett and Dave Evans, *Designing Your Life: How to Build a Well-Lived, Joyful Life* (New York: Knopf, 2016).

co-regulation is the basis for self-regulation. Deb Dana, *Anchored: How to Befriend Your Nervous System Using Polyvagal Theory* (Louisville, CO: Sounds True, 2021).

"you are the average of the five people." Jim Rohn, source unknown.

you are the average of ALL the people who surround you. David
      Burkus, *Friend of a Friend: Understanding the Hidden Networks
      That Can Transform Your Life and Your Career* (New York:
      Harper Business, 2018).
"lasting psychological connectedness between human beings." John
      Bowlby, *Attachment and Loss* (New York: Basic Books, 1969).
being aware of attachment styles can help regulate your nervous
      system. D.B. Drake, "Using Attachment Theory in Coaching
      Leaders: The Search for a Coherent Narrative," *International
      Coaching Psychology Review* 4, no. 1 (2009): 49–58.
your attachment style can change. R.C. Fraley, "Attachment in
      Adulthood: Recent Developments, Emerging Debates, and
      Future Directions," *Annual Review of Psychology* 4, no. 70
      (January 2019): 401–22.
"The difference between successful people and very successful
      people." Greg McKeown, *Essentialism: The Disciplined Pursuit
      of Less* (New York: Currency, 2014).
what attributes leaders would require for the future. Kim Schmidt,
      Joy Taylor, Anuj Kapoor, and Ramón Galcerán, "Changing
      Leadership in 2021 and Beyond," Grant Thornton website,
      March 18, 2021, grantthornton.global/en/insights/articles/
      Changing-leadership-in-2021-and-beyond/.
We need new ways to organize ourselves. Edward Morrison, Scott
      Hutcheson, Elizabeth Nilsen, Janyce Fadden, and Nancy Franklin,
      Strategic Doing: Ten Skills for Agile Leadership (Hoboken, NJ:
      Wiley, 2019).
We need to create spaces for deep, messy conversations. Burnett and
      Evans, *Designing Your Life*.
the need for leaders to attune to the conditions (including people)
      around them. Ginny Whitelaw, *Resonate: Zen and the Art of
      Making a Difference* (Virginia Beach, VA: Köehler Books, 2020).

Pillar 5: Trusting and Integrating Body Wisdom

"wholeness is not achieved by cutting off a portion of one's being."
      C. Sreechinth, *Musings of Carl Jung* (Google Books, 2018).

our two fundamental human needs as those of safety and of connection. Stephen Porges, *Polyvagal Safety: Attachment, Communication, Self-Regulation* (New York: Norton, 2021).

You form a template in your mind around trust. R. Lewicki and C. Brinsfield, "Trust as a Heuristic," in W.A. Donohue, R.G. Rogan, and S. Kaufman, *Framing Matters: Perspectives on Negotiation Research and Practice in Communication* (New York: Peter Lang Publishing, 2011).

the ingredients necessary for trust. Brené Brown, *Dare to Lead: Brave Work. Tough Conversations. Whole Hearts* (New York: Random House, 2018), 226.

"A settled body enables you to harmonize." Menakem, *My Grandmother's Hands*, 151–52.

Porges refers to this felt sense in the body as neuroception. Stephen W. Porges, "The Polyvagal Theory: New Insights into Adaptive Reactions of the Autonomic Nervous System," *Cleveland Clinic Journal of Medicine* 76, suppl. 2 (April 2009): S86–90.

a healthy dose of self-doubt can be grounding. Abhishek Rajput, "Why Self-Doubt Is an Important Trait for Leaders," LinkedIn, June 13, 2020, linkedin.com/pulse/why-self-doubt-important -trait-leaders-abhishek-rajput.

You stay in the mode of seeking knowledge. Baron Baptiste, *Being of Power: The 9 Practices to Ignite an Empowered Life* (Carlsbad, CA: Hay House, 2013).

"impostor syndrome"—self-doubt that cannot be justified by evidence. S. Feenstra, C.T. Begeny, M.K. Ryan, F.A. Rink, J.I. Stoker, and J. Jorgan, "Contextualizing the Impostor 'Syndrome,'" *Frontiers in Psychology* 11 (2020): 575024.

organizational cultures do not change overnight. Grant Freeland, "Culture Change: It Starts at the Top," Forbes.com, July 16, 2018, forbes.com/sites/grantfreeland/2018/07/16/culture-change -it-starts-at-the-top/?sh=59bc157a36c2.

everyone has a role to play in shifting the narrative. Brad Wayland, "Culture Change Is Bottom Up and Top Down," *TLNT*, April 1, 2019, tlnt.com/culture-change-is-bottom-up-and-top-down/.

you are often asked to "execute." Douglas Harper, "Etymology of
Execute," *Online Etymology Dictionary*, etymonline.com/word/
execute.

"each of you is perfect the way you are." Shunryu Suzuki, "Quotable
Quote," Goodreads, goodreads.com/quotes/249957-each-of-you
-is-perfect-the-way-you-are.

an equilibrium between your personal and work lives. Stewart D.
Friedman, Elizabeth Grace Saunders, Peter Bregman, and Daisy
Wademan Dowling, *HBR Guide to Work-Life Balance* (Brighton,
MA: Harvard Business Review Press, 2019).

Pillar 6: Finding Purpose and Contribution

what psychologist Angela Duckworth calls "grit." Angela Duckworth,
Grit: The Power of Passion and Perseverance (New York: Collins,
2018).

entrepreneur and professional coach Jerry Colonna. Jerry Colonna,
Reboot: Leadership and the Art of Growing Up (New York:
Harper Business, 2019).

Leading with Your Whole Self

"when you are authentic, you do not behave in toxic ways." Gabor
Maté, *The Myth of Normal: Trauma, Illness, and Healing in a
Toxic Culture* (New York: Avery Publishing, 2022).

"Nothing outside of you has changed." Judith Hanson Lasater,
Living Your Yoga: Finding the Spiritual in Everyday Life (Boulder,
CO: Shambhala Publications, 2015), 29.

About the Authors

Courtney Amo is the founder of Mahaa, an independent yoga, retreat, lifestyle coaching, and consulting practice that promotes inclusive and barrier-free access to well-being. With over twenty years of yoga teaching, public sector leadership, and facilitation experience, Courtney helps her students, team members, and colleagues approach work, life, and well-being from an embodied perspective. As a public sector leader, Courtney builds strong teams grounded in trust and respect, empowers team members to do their best work, and creates safe and inclusive work cultures. Courtney holds a bachelor of arts (honors) in psychology and a master of arts in education (measurement and evaluation) from the University of Ottawa, and she is a certified yoga instructor. She is also a certified Designing Your Life and Holobody coach, a Strategic Doing workshop leader, and a Zen Leadership practitioner. She has practiced yoga, meditation, and mindfulness for close to twenty-five years. When not spending time in nature, or with her husband and dogs in Moncton, New Brunswick, Courtney can be reached at Mahaa.ca.

Dr. Julie Beaulac is a registered clinical, health, and rehabilitation psychologist and consultant with a PhD in clinical psychology. She is bilingual, has worked in academic and hospital settings, is a certified yoga teacher, and teaches mindfulness. Julie's embodiment journey led her to start her own practice, which provides psychotherapy and consultation to individuals, groups, and organizations. A regular presenter at conferences across the globe and a published author in peer-reviewed journals, Julie is passionate about optimizing well-being and leadership through embodiment. She has worked for almost two decades to help clients enhance their performance and satisfaction by becoming more engaged in their lives. She lives in Ottawa and enjoys nature and being active outdoors, real food, connecting with people, and exploring Canada and abroad. Learn more about Julie at DrJulieBeaulac.com.

Casey Berglund is the founder of Worthy and Well, an online coaching and training company that helps founders, change-agents, and guides live their deeper purpose, become powerful Embodied Leaders, and get paid richly for the transformational work they are really here to do, without burning out or neglecting their bodies' wisdom. She has a bachelor of science degree in nutrition from the University of Alberta, is a 500-hour yoga instructor, certified professional coach, embodiment guide, TEDx speaker, and writer. Casey loves telling stories, teaching, and speaking with fascinating humans on *The Purpose Map*™ podcast and shares her more personal perspectives through her writing. She lives in Calgary, Alberta, but dreams of one day returning to a country lifestyle, with a couple of horses and a massive garden. You can learn more about Casey's work at LetYourBodyLead.com.

A Call to Action

THE MOST powerful way to use what you have learned is to take action. We encourage you to:

- **Share this book** with a friend, with your peers, or with your team. For more information on bulk purchases and discounts, please contact info@mindbodywaybook.com.

- **Share a post** of a key takeaway from this book on your social media and tag us at @MindBodyWayBook and #MindBodyWayBook.

- **Leave a review** on your online retailer of choice to connect the book with new readers.

- **Visit MindBodyWaybook.com** for more resources to support your embodied leadership journey and to stay informed about our work.

- **Ask us to speak or deliver a workshop** to you and your team. Please reach out at info@mindbodywaybook.com.

We honor you for embracing *The Mind-Body Way* and allowing it to support you in becoming a more Embodied Leader. Our wish is that this book continues to inspire and offer you incredible wisdom.

9 781774 583609